THRESHOLD EXPERIENCES

THRESHOLD EXPERIENCES
THE ARCHETYPE OF BEGINNINGS

MICHAEL CONFORTI, PhD

ASSISI INSTITUE PRESS
BRATTLEBORO, VERMONT

Published by:
Assisi Institute Press
Brattleboro Professional Center
PO Box 6033
Brattleboro, Vermont 05302 (USA)
Tel: (802) 254-6220
Web: www.assisiconferences.com

Cover & Layout Design:
Northern Cartographic
4050 Williston Road
South Burlington, Vermont 05403
www.ncarto.com

Printed in Canada
Text printed on acid free paper.

Library of Congress Cataloging-in-Publication Date Pending

DEDICATION

Per ogni bedda picciridda e beddu picciriddu stanno provando fare una vita, e attraversare il soglia da mondo visibile a il mondo eterno.

For each beautiful boy and girl trying to make a life and to cross the threshold from the visible world to the eternal world.

CONTENTS

FOREWORD

BY YORAM KAUFMANN, PH.D.

As science has evolved over time, it has become clear that what we know about our world, including ourselves, is to be found in the most unusual places. We have come to learn that information is holographic in nature; a small bit of knowledge can encompass the whole universe. A prominent example is DNA: every cell in our body contains information about our whole body. Theoretically, we can reconstruct the whole body from the information contained in the DNA of one cell. On a behavioral level, someone who is an expert in body analysis is able to draw an enormous amount of information about the personality of someone whom they are watching as they move; a gifted voice teacher can delineate your whole personality after hearing you sing, and so forth. In my doctoral studies I took a class in "listening" in which the teacher had us look at the first sentence a patient said after s/he came in, and we were supposed to infer from that how the session was going to progress. By focusing on a small piece of the puzzle it becomes possible to draw the complete picture.

I first met Michael Conforti as a student in my class at the C.G. Jung Institute in New York on the "Archetypes and the Collective Unconscious". It was a huge class. The students experienced me as a somewhat different teacher: I came in with an explicit methodology, demanding a different discipline, challenging the way most of them had approached the psyche. That aroused a lot of resistance, and created two unequal groups: the larger group, which found the material ranging from intimidating to unacceptable, and the smaller group, which found the material inspiring. Michael belonged to the latter, although not without some initial resistance. He began using the new way with the people he was teaching in Vermont, and had the experience of seeing it work where previous approaches had not. This emboldened him to come to me for supervision. The beginning was not auspicious. Michael presented a case where he was using an extreme form of an approach that led him to offer his analysand (patient) a twenty-minute interpretation, which, while possibly correct in contents could not but overwhelm the poor analysand. I was dumbfounded, and said, "This is horrendous, Michael." This kind of response would normally crush a supervisee, but, this being Michael, his reaction was quite different: he had on a big smile, and he said he was quite relieved. The authentic part of him knew that what he had been doing, while maybe correct on some level, was intrinsically inappropriate. Thus began our true relationship. What ultimately cemented it was his authenticity and genuineness, his open mind, his creative ways of looking at things, of integrating new approaches without losing his integrity. He was, in sum, the ideal student, and as all ideal students, he has surpassed his teacher and has ventured far afield, exploring new territories with daring, a sense of adventure, and insight.

In his book, *Threshold Experiences: the Archetype of Beginnings*, Dr. Conforti zooms in on a particular constellation: the critical moment of transition from one phase to another, or, to put it another way, on the initial conditions of a process, in particular, the psychotherapeutic encounter. Understanding of the crucial importance of initial conditions in determining the complete fabric of the process that follows has a long history in the physical sciences and in mathematics. Initial conditions play a prominent role in the study of partial differential equations, a special branch of mathematics that is useful in the study of systems that deal in the rate of change of several variables. A famous example is Maxwell's equations, by which Maxwell showed that electricity and magnetism are two sides of one phenomenon, electromagnetism, summarized by four partial differential equations. These equations have a myriad of solutions, some of them substantially different from one another. The important thing is that the nature of the solution is highly dependent on the initial conditions: different initial conditions lead to radically different solutions, and, therefore, describe radically different phenomena.

Another example that is of particular significance to humanity is our planet earth. According to several prominent scientists, the most fundamental problem facing our understanding of the world is why, given the hostile environments in the vast universe around us, is the planet earth friendly to humans (anthropic)? From what we know about cosmology today, it seems that all that was needed for life on earth, as we know it, to be impossible would have been a tiny change in the initial conditions after the Big Bang. For example, had the force of gravity been just slightly weaker or stronger, stars and planets would never had formed and living organisms (at least as we know them) would never have evolved. Our world is characterized by six constants. If any one of them were to be slightly different, life as we know it would not have been possible.

Initial conditions are, therefore, of fundamental importance. Dr Conforti demonstrates this idea by elegantly wending his way through example after example, exploring each instance by using an orientational approach, that is, amplifying each symbol by its essential dominants, and showing that this precise reading of the initial conditions leads to valid predictions about the outcome of the particular situation. In this way, he not only illustrates how crucial the initial conditions of a process are in determining how that process unfolds, he also demonstrates the most efficient way to examine and use those initial conditions, i.e., the orientational approach. In other words, Dr. Conforti illuminates both the "what" (initial conditions) and the "how" (orientational approach). Although this approach is particularly and dramatically applied here to dreams presented in a therapeutic encounter, it applies equally well to any beginning, and readers could profitably apply it to situations in which they were involved: the beginning of a relationship, the start of a physical construction, the onset of a professional training, etc. The manner in which the groom carries his bride over the threshold determines the nature of their marriage.

Yoram Kaufmann
Ramsey, February 12, 2007

T
H
R
E
S
H
O
L
D

E
X
P
E
R
I
E
N
C
E
S

FOREWORD

BY ROBERT LANGS, M.D.

I nitial conditions: My first contact with Michael Conforti was as one of his mentors. I was teaching a strongly adaptive approach to the emotion-processing mind and psychotherapy that brought therapists to the most telling but awesome and, at times, terrifying aspects of human emotional life. Many students were frightened off, but Michael stayed the course and made it a part of what was already shaping up to be an extremely broad and original view of the human psyche and its operations.

Over the years I have had the privilege of watching his thinking expand and grow in both scope and complexity. From the start, there appeared to be two key factors in his widening vision of the human condition and the psychotherapeutic healing process. The first lay with his natural ability to be both far-seeing and capable of integrating diverse sources of data and information into a viable whole. The second was his insight that Jung's concept of archetypes is, along with the idea of the unconscious mental processes, most basic to our comprehension of the emotion-related mind and its vicissitudes. Michael proceeded to take the concept of archetypal processes to new heights, using it as a guide to probing many biological and physical realms in order to garner insights that he then applied to the psychotherapeutic realm with a freshness that is seldom seen today.

As the trajectory of his work moved forward, in inevitable fashion, Michael transformed himself from my pupil to my teacher. As such, his unique gifts enabled him to be the kind of teacher whose ideas are not simply matters to be studied and memorized. Instead, he was and is a teacher of archetypes and universals that offers his audiences and readers the tools they need to build their own in-depth, operational view of the intricacies of human emotional life. This unique gift of his was there from the first moment I met Michael, and it is more than evident in these pages. I for one am quite grateful to be one of those to whom it has been given.

Robert Langs, M.D.

THRESHOLD

EXPERIENCES

INTRODUCTION

INITIAL CONDITIONS

The main part of this book was written twenty years ago as my graduation thesis for the C.G. Jung Institute of New York, and served also as part of my doctoral dissertation for Union Institute and University. At that time, I saw the thesis as a culmination of years of study, research and analytical practice. Looking back now, I see it not only as my graduate thesis, but also as a dynamic template from which all my future work could be intimated. I see now what I did not know then—how unseen forces within the psyche were guiding me toward a particular destiny.

I have allowed this publication of my doctoral thesis at the request of many students and colleagues who have wanted to observe the "initial conditions" of my work in much the same way I have wanted to observe and understand the "initial conditions" of the analytic dialogue. In this volume are the origins of questions I continue to find compelling. They contain the beginning of a pattern that has unfolded in increasing complexity and elegance throughout the last twenty years.

Many theorists have significantly informed my work, among them Dr. Robert Langs, a prolific author and major contributor to the disciplines of psychoanalysis and psychotherapy, and

Dr. Yoram Kaufmann, Jungian analyst and founder of the Orientational Approach. More on each of them is said below. But the primary influence in my work has been the unprecedented exploration into the structure and dynamics of the psyche which was the contribution of the late C.G. Jung, Swiss psychiatrist and younger contemporary of Freud, and founder of the School of Analytical Psychology.

Jung's original theme is that there is a destiny factor in a person's life, an *a priori* Self in potential, that insistently expresses itself throughout our lives. I believe that psychotherapy is not just about reading patterns; its fundamental goal is to articulate and understand the spirit that is already objectively present in someone's life in a profound way. Much of the material contained in this study draws upon Jung's idea of the objective psyche and his notion of the Self. Defining what was one of the key concepts in his psychology, Jung (1950) wrote:

> [There is] a centre of personality, a kind of central point within the psyche, to which everything is related, by which everything is arranged, and which is itself a source of energy. The energy of the central point is manifested in the almost irresistible compulsion and urge to become what one is, just as every organism is driven to assume the form that is characteristic of its nature, no matter what the circumstances. This centre is not felt or thought of as the ego but, if one may so express it, as the self. (¶ 634, p. 357)

In the Jungian view, the Self continually presents images, derivatives and dreams to the ego in hope of expanding and enhancing our conscious attitude. Jung's view of the Self thus implies the objective psyche, for it suggests an inborn set of determinants, and an innate understanding of how to achieve psychological health. It also involves a recognition that psyche and matter are two different aspects of one and the same thing. In the Jungian view, the Self is a unifying principle within the human psyche that occupies the central position of authority in relation to the psychological life and destiny of the individual.

Plato too believed that we are given our destiny at birth. He believed that our lives are shaped by an inherent intention, a *daimon* that guides the unfolding of life's events, and defines the meaning of our lives. To the extent that we live in conscious accordance with this potential "given-ness" of our particular nature, we seek to accomplish the pattern of our destiny that Jung called individuation.

The work of individuation demands the unraveling of the threaded knots of our families, hopes, careers, idiosyncrasies, relationships, acts of (occasional) madness, neurotic trends, spiritual longings, and moments of genius. Although individuation is a process of continuous discernment that is demanding, difficult and never finished, our attempt to be conscious of the seemingly isolated events, situations and encounters may eventually reveal an intricate pattern that conjoins the disparate parts into a coherent whole and shows the meaningful intention of a life fully lived. Eventually we may be able to look back into our beginnings and recognize how these early disparate events not only expressed our life then, but also hinted at the complexity of destiny's questions waiting to be answered.

It was probably my grandfather, Eugenio Conforti from Reggio, Calabria, Italy who first taught me how to visualize the future from the beginning. His expertise was with matter, not psyche, but the lessons he taught worked in both realms. He taught me how to make wine. From Grandpa I learned that the process begins with finding the best grapes. We tasted each bunch for their sweetness and tested their firmness. I learned that from our initial taste and impression of the grapes, an intimation of a future wine could be found. When the grapes were good and all of the steps in preparing the grapes and the barrels were ritualistically carried out, I discovered that my Grandpa could fortell the "destiny" of the wine's taste. As the barrels were sealed, he knew the taste which I could not know until the barrels were opened nine months later.

At its inception, the graduate thesis that has become this book began (like my early tutorial on wine) as a study of beginnings. It was conceived as a relatively straightforward project to study the unconscious dynamics of the Self in the beginning sessions of psychotherapy. A review of the literature at that time revealed that relatively little had been written on this subject. What was available addressed only the "how to's" for conducting the initial interview. The authors discussed issues such as: what to say to the client, what questions to ask, the imperative of listening to the patient's opening comments, issues concerning the timing of interpretations and other basic technical questions. Virtually nothing had been written about the unconscious dynamics operating within the initial interviews of psychotherapy, or the role of archetypes and/or the Self in structuring the dynamics within the patient-therapist relationship.

As I finished the literature review, I quickly realized that I had ventured into surprisingly unexplored clinical territory. I was curious about the reasons why the initial conditions of psychotherapy had not been seriously studied, and about the implications of its apparent omission. The absence of information sharply intensified my interest and research. I was attracted by this "black hole" in psychoanalytic theory.

The presence of that absence was compelling and became one of the most defining influences of my research. I felt as if some unknown door had opened as I entered into the Janus-faced world of what Jung had described as the psychoidal unconscious—the domain in which the psychological and the physical aspects of life are seen as two inextricable sides of a single coin. I wondered how the archetypal world influenced the manifestation of behaviors within the therapeutic dyad. At what point was it possible to see the archetype manifest in the therapy, and how could that information be used therapeutically?

In beginning this study, I was surprised by the lack of professional literature available about the unconscious influences in the initial interview. However, I gradually realized that it was the very absence of material that suggested the presence of something of great magnitude. I decided to approach the question analogically, to leave the psychic world and to look for similarities in the physical world. I remembered then that black holes in outer space were discovered because of a similar absence of matter. Where there appeared to be nothing, there was a significantly powerful, invisible something creating the field of apparent nothing. Black holes in outer space are formed by the concentration of intensely packed gravitational fields which pull matter into themselves, thus creating a vacuum, the illusion of empty, negative space.

Understood in this way, the negative space that defines black holes is really matter *in potentia*, intensely dense, invisible and with enormous gravitational pull. This same constellation of forces is present in any psychological complex, but to be a complex, the dynamism must be cloaked in a strong, consistent emotion that is disproportional to the stimulus event. Applying principles of black holes to the question of unconscious forces in analysis, I reasoned that the same pattern may exist regarding the scarcity of material about my dissertation topic. My argument suggested that there are powerful, illusive, and invisible influences that implicitly shape the dynamics of the analytic relationship and need to be recognized.

Once I determined that there are such unconscious influences operating within the therapeutic dyad, another question occurred: How would an understanding of their influence change the analyst's orientation to the process and focus of the analytic work? I began to wonder about the question of finding one's position within the world. Having been given a beautiful new compass, I recognized that a compass provides a sense of directionality—a way of locating oneself in the world. It helps to orient the user by locating Magnetic North. With that clarified, the user is then oriented in relationship to that position. The invariant presence of Magnetic North provides the basis for the compass's constant, from which those who use it can orient themselves.

Translating the language of the compass to that of the psyche, I reasoned that Magnetic North, as a point of orientation, finds its equivalent within the human psyche in the form of the objective psyche and the archetypes of the collective unconscious. Dr. Yoram Kaufmann, in *The Way of the Image*, describes these archetypal objectives or constants as "orientational markers", suggesting that a profound point of reference and inherent meaning exists within the psyche. These are archetypal dominants within the human psyche that work much like a compass to orient us to both the inner and outer worlds. C.G. Jung's extensive research on the structure and dynamics of the psyche spanned sixty years, seven languages, diverse cultures and personalities, and consistently pointed to the existence of archetypes—the structural, dynamic, *a priori*, invariant constants of the objective psyche.

The wisdom of both Drs. Jung and Kaufmann has been essential to my continuing research. Through my study, I have found that a serious inquiry into the nature of the initial conditions of treatment provides not only meaningful insights about the psyches of both patient and therapist, but also essential information about the manifestations of the archetypal processes responsible for the generation of form in the analytic relationship, in the pattern of the patient's life and in the outer, natural world. By focusing relentlessly on the initial conditions and frame issues in treatment, I came to recognize the inherent role of archetypes in determining how life is arranged, sequenced, and even generated in response to the presence of the innate, form-shaping, archetypal fields.

I realized that the actual form and patterns created within the patient/therapist relationship are orchestrated by the Self, functioning as a morphogenetic, form-producing field. Similar to the unfolding of form in the human embryo, whose dynamics cannot be fully understood through the prevailing biological paradigm, it appeared that some influence "seemingly" extrinsic to the temporal dynamics operative within these sessions was in fact responsible for the dynamics generated within them.

Matter, form and even life itself arise from a vast complex of dynamics, all of which speak both to the presence of innate ordering processes and to mysteries. My inner insistence on finding out about the influence of unseen forces on the development of form in the therapeutic relationship and in the lives of patients has led me in many academic directions: from psychology, to the sciences, to the spiritual domains, and to a journey into nature's ineffable world where the archetypal origins of matter, form, and design swirl about awaiting emergence and incarnation into the world of matter.

Not wanting to create yet another schism or duality, I worked to understand what these forces, energies and dynamics were and how they replicated in a fascinating series of interactions within the therapeutic setting, resulting in the creation of highly structured and archetypally interactive patterns. The field responsible for this form was not, as I had initially thought, extrinsic, but intrinsic to those fields responsible for the generation of form in therapy and life. Specifically, I was struck by the fact that the core issue in the client's life, such as abandonment, violence, incest, or other highly disturbing effects from their childhood, were re-enacted in the patient-therapist relationship, with a high degree of fidelity to the original trauma. Somehow, the past found its way into the current situation and seemed to influence the future trajectory of the treatment. To learn more about this phenomena, I turned to the early work of Freud (particularly in relation to his theory of repetition compulsion), to Theodore Reik's work on the "compulsion to repeat", and to the new sciences of emergence, to better understand these dynamics.

The shaping and intermingling of past, present and future is acknowledged by discoveries in the new sciences (which speak of a collapse of the space-time continuum). These observations also caused me to re-think commonly held notions about the role of memory. We can all agree that memory influences dynamics. Our past experiences tend to serve as the blueprint for current and future life events. So it may be safe to say that memory creates experience. As memories have the capacity to shape and guide our lives, I began to posit that memory is a reminder that we live in multiple worlds simultaneously. Memory serves to inform us of the presence of those fields which continue to shape our lives.

Roman Catholic theologians have long understood the presence of these eternal, ongoing fields. The concept of *anamnesis* captures the experience of being brought into a pre-formed, ongoing, active field. Citing the pivotal moments in the Mass, such as the Consecration and Transubstantiation, Jung agreed with the theologians that at those precise moments in the liturgy, the entire congregation is brought into an ongoing, archetypal drama (field), necessary to precipitate the congregation's emotional participation in these mysteries.

For Roman Catholics, this is not a ritualistic experience, but rather an immersion into something on-going. It is an experience of what anthropologist Levy-Bruhl called a *participation mystique* wherein the individual identity is temporarily eclipsed by the archetypal experience, and individuals are brought into an alignment with the numinous—a confrontation with the experience of transcendence. Within this experience lies one of the central bridges uniting ancient wisdom about what Jung understood as the *unus mundus* (the one world), to the "unified field" studied by Einstein and other theoretical physicists. Persons who have such numinous experiences often relate feelings of unity with the cosmos, or feelings of ecstatic wholeness. Modern terms from quantum physics and chaos theory echo the ideas of mystical unity. Concepts such as String Theory, Entanglement, and Interpenetrability all speak to this underlying, transcendent, interconnected reality.

For more than twenty-five years my professional life has been compelled by the need to answer a single question: "What is it that has the capacity to structure and influence matter, and guide it into seemingly pre-formed states?" I understood that for the answer to evolve, I had to study the dynamic presence of fields in both the individual psyche and the outer, natural world.

A number of central influences emerged during this period that helped shape the advancement of these ideas. They included Dr. Yoram Kaufmann's work on the objective image, Dr. Robert Lang's findings that psychotherapy itself is an operative, bi-personal field, Dr. Rupert Sheldrake's work on morphogenetic fields, Dr. Fred Abraham's study of fields determining their own trajectories, Dr. Ervin Laszlo's idea that "field precedes form", and biophysicist Dr. Beverly Rubik's work on the bio-field. Additionally, my work was enhanced by understanding Dr. Brian Goodwin's capacity to see organisms and mind as one interconnected system, Dr. Mae-wan Ho's insights into "coherent systems," Dr. Adolph Portmann's work on prefigured, non-local biological fields, Dr. Joan Chodorow's innovative work on movement and emotions, and Elie Wiesel's profound explication of the Hassidic and Judaic wisdom traditions. Each in his or her own way and from within their own respective disciplines augmented a developing understanding of the workings of the Self within the initial conditions of therapy and the emergence of life on the micro and macroscopic levels.

It was during my second year of training at the C.G. Jung Institute in New York, that I truly learned to appreciate the workings of the objective psyche and of the innate meanings embedded within its images. Dr. Yoram Kaufmann, who was originally trained as a physicist in his native Israel prior to training as a Jungian analyst, provided what I believe is one of the most brilliant and disciplined approaches to archetypes and the objective psyche.

For Jung and the first generation of Jungians, the primacy of the archetype was recognized to be of tremendous psychological importance. Since then we have seen a steady movement by latter-day Jungians away from the objective, *a priori* nature of the archetypal image, to a perspective that stresses the primacy of the individual's feelings and thoughts about the image. I call this latter approach a subjective, relativistic perspective. In other words, while Jung and the early Jungians sought to understand images and life circumstances from the vantage point of innate, eternal, archetypal processes, much of the contemporary practice of Jungian analysis has diminished the appreciation of the objective psyche and moved toward an emphasis on the subjective, personal relationship to the image. The consequence of this subjective, relativistic approach suggests that the archetypal image should be eclipsed by a subjective appropriation of meaning, which in my opinion misaligns the ego/Self axis and leads toward the arrogance of ego-inflation, away from the moral process of individuation.

During my early work with Dr. Kaufmann, I quickly realized the importance and repeated accuracy of his approach to images. In addition, I sensed that another step had to be taken in order to better understand the underlying, generative domain from which these images arose. I felt that the image needed to be viewed as part of the mosaic of a larger, archetypal pattern. While Kaufmann stressed the meaning of the image, I became equally interested in the ground from which the image emerged and began to conceive of a theory in which the image was seen as an expression, explication, representation and incarnation of a pre-existing archetypal field.

Shortly thereafter, I developed an interest in the dynamics occurring within therapeutic interactions. Specifically, through a series of experiences both with candidates in training and in supervision with senior analysts, I realized that a majority of our cases reflected as much about the clinician's psyche as it did about the patient's. Sensing yet another thread in this complex knot of my interest in self-organizing systems, I followed these observations and insights, which led me to the doorstep of the gifted and iconoclastic Freudian psychoanalyst, Robert Langs.

I arranged for a supervisory consultation with Dr. Langs, and can still vividly recall the details of that initial interview. Prior to this first session, he had asked me to prepare a verbatim account of a recent session. Fortunately I had just completed a session where I was totally baffled by the material, and decided to present that for supervision. I presented Langs with the clients most recent dream: "I am driving down the highway and see trees being pulled out by their roots."

Totally perplexed by the dream, I asked for Langs's opinion. Without hesitation, he explained that the image captured an abortion experience—something alive being pulled out by the roots—the effects of which both the client and therapist remained unaware and unconscious. I had no knowledge of my patient's having had any abortions, but nevertheless was struck by the way Langs worked with the image. Upon seeing the client the following week, she suddenly volunteered that prior to the last session, she had just undergone her fifth abortion. I was struck not only by the pain she was beginning to feel in addressing the abortion issue, but also with Langs's insights about the dream's imagery.

It was Langs's insistence on the fidelity of the image to the experience and his ability to infer the experience that preceded the image that particularly caught my interest. In retrospect, this experience helped in developing for myself an archetypal field theory. From it, I began to understand the implicit relationship not only between the image and experience, but also between field and form. In this regard, I could see how form is the expression of the field from which it has emerged. Conversely, I understood that the material, symbolic expression of form (and by extension, its images) are constrained by the nature of the field itself. Here I saw the wonderful confluence of field and form, and the possibilities of making relatively accurate interpretations (not only about the past, from form to field), but also about how a future could be inferred from the present.

Similar to Kaufmann's approach, Langs's work represents a deep regard for underlying structure, and an artful and disciplined approach to psyche. They both understand that unconscious, archetypal experiences are captured in the precision of our language and images.

Langs is most widely recognized for his work on the therapeutic frame and the workings of a bi-personal, patient-therapist interactional field. Specifically he views the therapeutic dyad as an entity unto itself, within which each member provokes and reacts to the other's dynamics within the bi-personal field. Sensing that some greater agency was at work in these interactions, I later realized that in addition to Langs's causal explanation of field phenomena, that there was a form-shaping, archetypal field responsible for the dynamics unfolding within the patient-therapist dyad. Similar to the influence of morphogenetic fields in the unfolding of human life, I began to understand the generation of form within the therapeutic experience as being carefully crafted by a series of universal regularities that govern the progression of its formation.

Thoughts about this issue reached a crescendo during Dr. Langs's 2005 presentation at the Assisi, Italy Conference. In that lecture, he described a situation wherein a client missed a session, and the therapist called later that day to see what had happened. Appreciating the analyst's concern, the client indicated that she would explain everything at the next session. When she arrived for the next appointment, she once again expressed her appreciation for the analyst's thoughtfulness, and then proceeded to describe her terrible marital problems, in which her reportedly paranoid husband accused her of being involved in an affair, and had her followed by a private detective. She went on to say that he stalked her wherever she went, and would not leave her alone.

Langs made an excellent interpretation of this material saying that in the same way the husband had been stalking her, the therapist, by calling her about the missed appointment, had assumed a similar role to the husband's. This interpretation was based on Langs's thoughtful rendering of the client's unconscious communication. While I believe this was an accurate accounting of the material, I felt there was much more to learn about the nature of the human interaction depicted in this clinical event, specifically about the stunning fidelity of the replication of interaction occurring in life and in treatment.

This case exemplifies the issue I had begun to understand, that the therapeutic situation itself functions as an attractor site (a Magnetic North) drawing attention to the patient's complex that needs to be explored. In Dr. Langs's case study, some degree of enactment seemed necessary in order for there to be any integration and for resolution to occur. It appeared that the issue itself (and the field from which it was generated) exerted an influence that created the conditions for the re-enactment. Entrance into the inherently choreographed therapeutic dance represents an invitation to engage in a highly orchestrated interaction, requiring the syncopated movements, dialogue and activity of each party to bring to the present an event held in potential within an archetypal field.

However as previously mentioned, memory is not a static, fixed point in history, but a vital, determining shaper of individual and collective experience. I soon realized that while these experiences occurred within the context of an individual life, the pattern of events themselves was timeless.

"Once upon a time", begins many a fairy tale. The phrase captures the essential timelessness of archetypal stories. For instance, in my own clinical work I may have been seeing and unknowingly participating in a re-enactment of the story of abandonment (when working with a patient orphaned at birth). I now began to understand that the behaviors, tendencies and needs of an individual coming from this background represent the behaviors of the 'orphan' archetypal field itself.

While feelings and emotions are experienced individually, they remain nevertheless essentially universal in nature, in that the archetype (in this case being orphaned) is recorded like an energic Platonic Ideal embedded within the psyche that precedes and predicates the individual's psychological experience. I saw that behaviors and proclivities embedded within historical, archetypally-driven events could often determine the trajectory both of a life and of a therapeutic system.

This idea of field generating form and experience is aptly described by Fred Abraham, a renowned mathematician and chaos theorist, who explains that trajectories are determined by the field, and that the confines of these fields remain relatively constant because of the presence of a stable attractor. In the case we are imagining, we can view the 'orphan' archetype as the attractor determining the form of the experience. He goes on to say that instabilities and change occur as there is a shift from one to another attractor site. Herein lies a clear understanding of the stabilities of fields and behaviors evidenced while under the influence of these archetypal attractors.

Once again, my course of inquiry led back to ideas about the existence and dynamics of pre-formed fields (morphogenetic stabilities) which worked to entrain each member of the system into its orientation. I wondered if there could really be something as powerful as a field to structure form (and in the case of therapeutic interactions), guide the unfolding interaction between two people?

Mounting evidence stemming from disciplines as diverse as biophysics, developmental biology and Jung's archetypal psychology, suggested that this indeed was the case. In studying the biological domain I had learned that genetics and DNA play a large role in the generation of human form. However, as Rupert Sheldrake, D'Arcy Thompson and C.W. Waddington all suggest, form is not simply the result of biological processes but is a phenomena invoking the powers of generative, form-shaping fields. In the outer, natural world, we find influences such as gravitational, magnetic and electrical fields as powerful shapers of form (think of magnets and iron filings).Explorations of the new sciences into the domains of matter now provide us with correlates to the workings of psyche, in much the same way that alchemy provided a material correlate for Jung's research.

Building on these ideas, I studied Robert Becker's investigations of electromagnetic fields and the work of Lawrence Fagg, a nuclear physicist and theologian, who in *Electromagnetism and the Sacred,* posits that electromagnetic fields are the generative source of life itself. Each provided evidence for the role of electromagnetic fields and forces in the regeneration of form in animals such as the salamander, starfish and newt.

Later, I discussed the correlation between electromagnetism and archetypal fields via the study of the work of Dr. Ervin Laszlo, the renowned philosopher of science, systems theorist and author of more than 350 books and articles on the interconnected universe. Dr. Lazlo felt that my correlation between the workings of archetypes and fields in the outer world was an important insight, but one that could be only partially correlated. He indicated that although the workings of electromagnetic fields are space-time dependent, (i.e. the closer the magnet is to the object, the stronger its influence) he recognized archetypes and archetypal fields as non-local and independent of the same space-time constraints experienced by fields in the outer, natural world.

Laszlo's comments opened yet another door for my work in this area. As I realized that discoveries in the traditional and new sciences could provide further insights into this domain, I decided to enter the world of chaos theory and theoretical physics.

In that bizarre, topsy-turvy world of the new sciences and quantum physics, psyche lives in the domain of invisible, psychoidal, non-deterministic processes, where fields, form, and dynamics all exist as potentialities. Entering an Alice-in-Wonderland world, where the prevailing ways for apprehending reality fail us miserably, I needed another lens, another guide to traverse these waters.

The new sciences and Jung's extensive study of the objective psyche combined to provide such a lens. Each discipline delves more deeply into the very nature of life itself, and into the processes responsible for the generation of life and meaning. Each speaks of eternal processes, and about a way of seeing that transcends contemporary consciousness. Each presented me with the collective wisdom of humanity's experience.

Throughout history, pilgrims who traverse the terrain of life's mysteries are required to accept a way of knowing that has been granted only to those known as the "wise ones" in every culture. Traditionally, the wise ones' knowledge transcends the level of our everyday world of conscious reality and sees past the dialectics of usual consciousness into the infinite world of archetypal wisdom. I realized that in order to glimpse the world the wise ones see so clearly, an orientation to knowledge of a very different nature was required. I needed to study the wisdom traditions to learn something about the vital secrets preserved in the canons of the world's greatest spiritual works.

From that reading and research, I came to recognize that Jung's theory of archetypes provides a contemporary framework for our experience of the sacred. Like Jung, I am convinced that archetypes have the capacity to shape life and phenomena, and to draw us into the deepest spiritual layers of the psyche. Archetypal theory thus serves as a bridge to the traditions of eternal wisdom, allowing us to see and know something about the fundamental truths of human experience that sages have known since the beginning of time.

I arrived at this realization while reading Elie Wiesel's autobiography, *And the Sea Is Never Full.* He is a brilliant man whose greatest gift is his life—the story of a man who has not only seen, but also lived in the "other world" of Nazi atrocities and came back to tell us about it. Since that first reading, I have been absorbed in his work and that of other Jewish scholars. From Wiesel, to Martin Buber, to writers on the early Hassidic traditions, Rabbi Zalman Schachter-Shalomi and Abraham Joshua Heschel, I have read and am learning. They all seek to put into words the ineffable experiences of being human. Their words, visions and ideas from this sacred world remind us that human experience is grounded in and governed by the archetypal world. I have come to realize that this spiritual, mystical body of literature is as fundamental to our study of psyche as are the readings of psychological theory, the world's mythologies, fairy tales and alchemical texts. Each transports us beyond the veil of our known reality and into the mysteries that matter. Jung's pioneering work, the on-going dialogues within psychoanalytic theory, the discoveries in the new sciences, and the wisdom of the sages all whisper secrets about the depth of the human spirit that reside within and beyond us all.

To know of wisdom is to have been mentored, and to be mentored by one of the "wise ones" is truly a gift. Elie Wiesel had the good fortune to have found a mentor, Rabbi Saul

Lieberman, considered by many to be one of the worlds greatest Talmudic scholars. In his hunger to better understand and experience this realm of wisdom, Wiesel found in Rabbi Lieberman the mentor, master, and initiator into this domain of sacred literature, and the guide into and through this life journey, he so desperately needed.

In writing about this relationship, Wiesel states:

> Who was he for me? A major intellectual influence, a source of knowledge that his peers admired? Much more. He was to me a Master, a guide, a support. And something else. He was my great friend....His judgment was sure, always based on a knowledge that never ceased to surprise me....Faithful to what he conceived as the primary truth...he hated banality and showed himself to be intolerant to mediocrity that he did not mind denouncing mercilessly. (Lubetski, 2002, p. 2)

I have been extraordinarily fortunate to have found Yoram Kaufmann and Robert Langs during this journey, who not only taught me the skills needed to have a life, but at the appropriate times, have encouraged me to live my life beyond its limits. I am thankful for their genius and generosity, and consider my life blessed by their scholarship and friendship. This book is the result of many of these early questions and dialogues. It represents the early, seedling questions of my career as an analyst that have led me to a life of continuous study that remains an insatiable drive.

At my editor's insistence, I have agreed to comment on my more recent history and the developments of the Assisi Institute and Assisi Conferences. In addition to my analytic practice, I now serve as an organizational consultant, mentor, writer, teacher, clinical supervisor, film consultant and President of the Assisi Institute, which offers a certificate program for Archetypal Pattern Analysts. The Institute was born last year in response to increasing requests for training articulated by what has become known as the "Assisi Community", a diverse, multi-talented, welcoming group of more than 20,000 people who have been attracted to the work I continue to do and to love.

It has been extraordinarily humbling and satisfying to see the influence this work has had on professionals from so many different fields over the past twenty-five years. As this work continues to reach beyond its original borders of psychotherapy and analysis, it is now influencing not only therapists, but also artists, legal professionals (in particular the work of a colleague who for many years as a Superior Court Judge oversaw death sentencing cases); museum exhibitors, photographers, educators (seeking to bring an awareness of the reality of the psyche and its patterns to the classroom); organizational consultants (bringing a new vision of coherence and an articulation of archetypal dominants in organizational life); clergy, seeking to better understand the archetypal roots of clergy abuse; international peace negotiators; and recently my own involvement consulting for directors, producers and screenwriters to determine the archetypal coherence of film scripts.

This work has crossed not only professional but also geographical boundaries. Archetypal pattern analysis is now practiced by colleagues and students in Denmark, Italy, Canada, Venezuela and Switzerland, as well as the United States. In addition, the body of work that I have produced over the last twenty-five years anchors the core curriculum for the Assisi Institute's Training Program in Archetypal Pattern Analysis.

A number of years ago I had the good fortune to have Dr. James Hollis introduce me to an audience in Assisi, Italy. His words were kind when he stated that the passion driving my work was a good example of what the ancients called Divine Madness. I know I have lived (and occasionally suffered) both sides of that designation. The insistent need to push ever deeper into familiar territory and to look into totally alien corridors for insights and answers suggests the presence of an insatiable inner *daimon*, which continues to shape and give meaning to my life. It is clear that the work is neither done, nor the destination reached. A next book (on complexes) is being readied for publication.

I want to thank the following individuals who have provided unwavering (and insistent) support, criticism, and care for the completion of this project and for my ongoing investigations. From the bottom of my heart, I want to thank my son, Christopher Conforti, who constantly reminds me about the power of the image, and the strength needed to make a good life. My friend and colleague, Diane Antczak, who has read this manuscript many times. Each time, she has taken a word or phrase and transformed it into something special. Thank you. Ann Lammers, who jumped in at the 11th hour to offer invaluable editorial assistance with this work. Janet Brown, clinician, scholar, friend and colleague who edited this present volume. With the eye of an artist, she has shaped this book into a thoughtful and engaging read. As a grower of dahlias, she knows of beauty and what is needed to bring it to fruition. Like a gardener sensing fertile soul beneath the rubble of time, she worked with this material and found a way to bring out its best. Thank you, thank you, Jan.

I sense I may have written more than was needed in this retrospective introduction. If this is the case, I ask for your indulgence. I am Italian. When you visit our homes, there is always too much to eat, too many different dishes, and we tend to leave the table with bellies too full. However, for an Italian, the meal is an expression of the love for the guests and for the ritual of the dinner, in which each course of each meal is prepared with the utmost care in order to give something special from one's heart to those around the table.

To my readers and friends, Buon Appetito!

Michael Conforti, Ph.D., March 2007

Brattleboro, Vermont

NOTE FROM THE EDITOR

PRESERVING THE WORK'S
INITIAL CONDITION

This thesis by Dr. Michael Conforti was written in 1988 in completion of his doctoral studies at Union Institute and University, and his graduation thesis at the C.G. Jung Institute of New York. "It examines," he writes, "the initial psychotherapy interview situation through the presentation of historical, developmental, and clinical material, in an effort to explain why many patients are so acutely sensitive to the conditions of treatment." Secondly, he said, "it offers a perspective for comprehending patients' unconscious communication in the first session and the beginning phase of treatment." It is an aggressive, courageous piece of scholarship written with the insistent energy of a young man's compelling curiosity and passion for understanding the psyche. This first major work sits like an index intuitively cataloguing Dr. Conforti's future accomplishments as an internationally recognized analyst, educator, author, lecturer, consultant and founder of the Assisi Institute for the Study of Archetypal Pattern Analysis. In order to preserve the energy and style of the original thesis, editing for its retrospective publication has been intentionally spare.

Janet D. Brown, January 2006, Hollis, NH

Dissertation Introduction

Premise and Content

Little has been written about the importance of the initial interview and preliminary phase of treatment for the patient beginning psychotherapy. Works such as Sullivan (1954) *The Psychiatric Interview* and Deutsch and Murphy (1955a) *The Clinical Interview* describe the technical procedures needed to ensure a successful initial consultation. However, these and other works on the subject, such as Freud (1913) neglect discussing the underlying reasons why the first treatment session is of such vital importance to the success of the analysis.

Studies examining patients' unconscious communications about the therapist and the therapeutic setting have been recorded by Goodheart (1984b), Langs (1985), Little (1981), Searles (1979), and Blomeyer (1980). Blomeyer, a Jungian analyst, studied how the patient unconsciously incorporates the therapist into himself, and documented how these experiences were evidenced in the patient's material. Describing the unintended, unconscious power of the therapist to affect the responses of child patients, Blomeyer comments on the surprising results of the unconscious influence of two therapists on drawings done by children in therapy: "Certain candidates (analysts in training) unconsciously constellated similar elements in content and structure in different children and adolescents..." (p. 20).

He also states:

The results brought about equally contradictory reactions in me... It should simply not be true that nine out of fifteen of Gert's children, and ten out of twenty of Anke's, have made drawings with the same characteristic manner, and that this may be traced back to the specific shadings emanating from the investigator. (p. 28)

Although Blomeyer's work addressed children's unconscious responses to treatment, I felt that his findings could be helpful when examining adults' response to the initial interview situation. Stimulated by Blomeyer's research, I wanted to determine what personal and archetypal factors were responsible for patients' intense response to the unconscious dynamics of treatment. This question led me into the study of mother/infant interactions, because it articulates the individual's first experience of relationship and of having to respond to another's (the mother's) psyche. I looked at how significantly the quality of the mother/infant dyad affects the child, and similarly how the psychological well-being of the analyst affects the patient. I also examined how the analyst's capacity to maintain the analytic structure affects the patient and the outcome of the analysis. I discovered that in the same way that children express their unconscious reactions and perceptions of the maternal environment, patients also express their (unconscious) perceptions of the qualities of the therapeutic setting.

As a way into these questions, I examine the archetypal roots of the therapeutic relationship, via accounts of healing rites from the Asklepieions in Chapters 1 and 2. The importance of the actual location for the healing site is repeatedly stressed throughout this ancient historical account, and is explored as directly relevant to the particular formation of the therapeutic relationship. This chapter shows how modern psychotherapy is influenced and structured by the same dynamics and practices found in these eternal healing practices.

Realizing the profound effect the actual site and the container of healing have for those seeking help, I began to look with fresh eyes, upon the nature of mother-infant interactions in Chapter 3. In addition to the importance of the mother-child interactions and the archetypal aspects of the therapeutic environment, a third theme within this thesis is the effect that early (especially traumatic) experiences have on the formation of the individual's life. Included in this discussion are the various ways in which patients recreate their early experiences within the analysis. Studying the life-long effects of trauma on infants, Greenacre (1952) writes: "These traumata may in themselves be the predominantly determining experiences for later forms of ... expression, but in any event never occur without some of the earlier elements" (p. 20). Discussing the phenomenon of reliving traumatic experiences in the analytic relationship, Freud (1915) writes:

He [the patient] is obliged to repeat the repressed material as a contemporary experience instead of ... remembering it as something belonging to the past. These reproductions... are invariably acted out in the sphere of the transference, of the patient's relation to the physician. (p. 20)

In chapters 4 and 5, I discuss Jung's discovery of the Word Association Test, and the subsequent development of his theory of the complex, which may stand as one of his greatest contributions. Then I move on to an investigation of Jung's actual work with patients in the initial interview.

In the clinical examples presented in Chapters 6 and 7, I demonstrate that patients do tend to recreate their earlier traumatic experiences within the analysis. However, what is not described in the analytic literature is the extent to which analysts unknowingly assist in the recreation of the traumatic episodes through their willingness to accept and create special conditions of treatment. These special conditions are either requested by patients or are created by the analyst in constructing the framework of the therapy. I have found the tendency to repeat or to recreate the traumatic experience to be in full force during the initial interview. If it is not understood or carefully analyzed, it can significantly impede analytic progress.

Chapter 8 represents my earliest inroads into the areas of innate ordering processes and the new sciences as it examines the underlying ground from which form and process emerge. Drawing on the work of Rupert Sheldrake and contributions from the fields of morphogenetic studies, I laid the foundation for what was to subsequently evolve into my theory of archetypal fields. A summation of my findings about the archetypal underpinnings within the initial interview is presented in Chapter 9.

The Appendix includes a paper representing my early investigations into chaos theory and the workings of attractor sites as a shaper of phenomena within the clinical situation. Drawing on a family therapy session, this paper presents my research team's findings relevant to the evolving field of emergence.

CHAPTER 1

ARCHETYPAL IMAGES OF HEALING
AND THE THERAPEUTIC PROCESS

S tudying both ancient and contemporary ways that physicians meticulously attend to clinical details in the practice of healing and medicine can inform therapists about the necessity for giving conscious consideration to all facets of the therapeutic relationship, including how the therapist interacts with patients and the manner in which the therapeutic setting is created and maintained. I have been struck by how patients' unconscious communications in the initial interview often record strong emotional configurations in response to the conditions of treatment.

This phenomenon has raised for me the question: Is there an archetypal reason for patients' demonstrating such a great sensitivity to the conditions of treatment? To answer this question, I have researched accounts of ancient healing practices, paying special attention to the details of healing experiences from the Asklepienion traditions. Kerényi's (1947) *Asklepios* and Meier's (1967) *Ancient Incubation and Modern Psychotherapy* have been especially useful resources in the descriptions of ancient healing practices. Much of this literature contains references to the actual conditions of treatment, the procedures used by the physicians, and in virtually every account, the importance of the healing site.

Healing rites have occupied a central position in the history of human development. Our fascination with healing originates not only from a need to ensure physical survival, but also from our desire to maintain a relationship with the divine. Originally, sickness was believed to result from a person's falling out of grace, a loss of contact with one's spiritual nature. Much of the healing process was an attempt to bring the patient back into relationship with his or her soul.

The descriptions of healing rites provide a great deal of emphasis on the specific practices and procedures used by the physician. Although unique approaches to cures differed from region to region, a number of central practices are shown to have been used universally, including the careful selection of the healing site, purification rituals, and the invocation of a higher force to induce the cure.

The fact that a number of healing rites and practices have achieved such widespread usage may be attributed to the fact that they represent habitual, archetypally-derived modes of cure, encoded into the collective unconscious in much the same way that morphogenetic processes are encoded into a species. There is an archetype of the healing relationship, complete with its own set of unconscious dictates and mandates, and we now find that a study of these practices sheds light on the archetypal dynamics of healing and the current therapeutic situation. Further, I believe these ancient practices are applicable in the modern therapeutic relationship, and are especially important in the initial interview situation.

In *Asklepios*, Kerényi (1947) presents the following picture of the god's birth: "On Koronis's pyre Asklepios was born: Apollo delivered the child from the dead mother" (p. 19).

Asklepios's life was intimately related to death: his birth and his mother's death were simultaneous. Eliade (1964) points out that many, if not all, of the young men chosen as apprentice shamans had physical deformities or near-death experiences during their youth. Living with sickness and developing a conscious relationship to it prepared healers to face their patients' suffering. A second aspect of having faced death is that it alerts the individual to the existence of a transpersonal force. For instance, a child who has seen his or her parent struggle with debilitating disease or death, will unconsciously understand that there are forces in life that govern our existence, and perhaps even our destiny, and are far beyond our control. Such an experience represents an early encounter with the power of the unconscious.

After his mother's death, Asklepios was suckled by an animal. Thus, the mothering object shifts from a human to a non-human form, suggesting that Asklepios found nurturance and sustenance in the instinctual and transpersonal realms, and not solely from the world of the personal.

Asklepios's reliance on the archetypal mother can be translated as a necessary therapeutic attitude, that is, therapeutic success will be achieved only when the Self contributes to the analytic process. Reliance on archetypal energies is evidenced in the analytic setting when the clinician listens to patient's unconscious material presented through dreams and derivatives, both of which are products of a non-ego sector of the personality. A correlation between Asklepios's relationship with the personal and archetypal mother, may be evidenced in the therapeutic relationship as the clinician's attention to both the personal/manifest level ego-oriented material and the latent/derivative archetypal dimensions of meaning. Kerényi continues his study of Asklepios by discussing the process used for choosing the actual sites for the Asklepienions. He describes the selection of the Tiber Island site:

> The ancients picked their cult sites on the basis of religious meaning. The terrain [of the Tiber Island] was so low lying that special measures were frequently required to prevent it from becoming a morass. The Tiber Island was a place of considerable religious significance: according to the Roman tradition, it was originally a floating island.... After the

island formed, it was consecrated to Faunus, the ancient Italic wolf god. For Faunus signifies 'strangler'... he was wilder and had about him something of the beast of prey, expressing the wolf-like quality of the all-devouring darkness. (p. 16)

A number of significant features emerge from this description. They are:

1. special measures had to be used to keep the island from flooding

2. it had originally been a floating island

3. it was consecrated to Faunus, the wolf-god.

The special measures taken to keep the island from flooding symbolize and speak to the delicate nature of the relationship between conscious and unconscious experience within the therapeutic situation. The work requires the analyst to carefully assess how much unconscious material the patient's ego can effectively handle during analysis, lest the eruption of unconscious contents "flood" the patient's conscious functioning.

The fact that the Tiber healing site is located on an island is an important symbolic reference, which refers to an unconscious content existing independent of ego consciousness. Jung (1954, 1953) discusses the dual nature of island symbolism in the following passages:

...the patient needs an island and would be lost without it. It serves as a refuge for his consciousness and as the last stronghold against the ever-threatening embrace of the unconscious.... (p. 181)

The purpose of the descent as universally exemplified in the myth of the hero is to show that only in the region of danger (watery abyss, cavern forests, islands, and castles) can one find the treasure hard to attain...the victory over death. (p. 335)

On the one hand, the island represents the place to which patients flee when faced with threatening unconscious material.

On the other hand, the patient has to travel to the island to find the meaning of whatever psychic content has been shipwrecked there. Both meanings indicate the importance of island imagery for developing and maintaining relations between the ego and unconscious experience in the beginning phases of treatment. The island is a rich symbol indicating a solid entity–an archetype–existing within the sea of the collective unconscious. It is often a place of special value and requires some degree of navigation both to arrive at and to leave. The island's dedication to Faunus, the strangler, signifies the healing site's relationship to death. A possible reason for choosing an island and dedicating it to Faunus has to do with an understanding that healing necessitates ego death. Coming face-to-face with the threat of annihilation represents key moments in the process of ego-Self development. When death looms large, the ego is suddenly seen as small and fragile, and the person begins to understand the immense power of the unconscious.

The numerous accounts of divine intercession in patients' dreams while in treatment at the Asklepienion underscore the concern over finding the proper location for the healing site. The ancients' medical and spiritual procedures had to be followed with strict religious devotion because the entire healing experience was geared toward reaching an epiphany—that moment when a god appeared to heal the patient. The priests understood that both the inner and outer conditions of treatment, as well as the inner and outer conditions of the patient, had to be synchronized and arranged in correspondence with the archetype of healing. Both were necessary to establish a psychologically receptive state within a particular environment in order to create a situation in which the ancient gods could effect their cure—or in modern terms, in which the elements of the psyche could effect a cure.

The same attention to detail exercised in choosing the healing site was also employed by ancient physicians in their work with patients. In *The Healing Hand: Man and Wound in the Ancient World*, Majno (1975) conducts a "complete history of the wound" and healing practices. The following is a description of the physicians' art, taken from the Hippocratic Collection (400 B.C.E):

> *The physician himself, though not aseptic, was spotless, neat, and reassuring-even perfumed.... Even his posture in the operating had to be elegant. If he stands, he should make the examination with both feet fairly level, but to operate, with the weight on one foot (not that on the side of the hand in use). When seated, his feet should be in a vertical line straight up as regards his knees, and be brought together with a slight interval. (p. 148)*

An essential aspect of the (psychological) healing experience today is that both patient and therapist understand the terror, fear, joy and numinosity present in the contents of the unconscious. The axiom "only the wounded healer heals" echoes many of the images of Asklepios-his suffering, his relationship to death, and his profound awareness of the transpersonal. Kerenyi (1947) writes: "The eyes [of Asklepios] seem to look upward and into the distance without a definite aim. This, combined with the vivid movements, gives us an impression of a great inner emotion, one might say, almost of suffering" (p. 2).

In treatment, any attempt on the part of the therapist or patient to avoid this encounter with the unconscious must be carefully analyzed and rectified.

Therapists' fear of the analytic situation is stressed by Rhally (1968), a Jungian analyst, who writes:

> *...an attitude of absolutely having to offer something, whether it be cigarettes or sweets, pills, or answers, mostly serves to protect the therapist from the intensity of the unsated hunger of the patient or from his negative transference. It is easy to observe just those therapists who constantly want to help, who actually ignore or even discourage the patient's cry for help....If the therapist gets onto this level, in my opinion, he is already through. For he has thereby retreated from the encounter with the patient. (pp. 225, 227)*

The Asklepieion model of treatment encouraged patients to look to unconscious/divine intervention for guidance. Remnants of this ideal are practiced when the analytic environment turns its attention to unconscious material, and to the manifestations of the Self and its attempt to guide the healing process.

CHAPTER 2

ARCHETYPAL DYNAMICS OF THE ANALYTIC SETTING AND ITS IMPLICATIONS FOR THE INITAL INTERVIEW

Beneath all images of the container (i.e. the therapeutic vessel, the holding environment, the cave, the abyss, the earth, and the womb) lies an archetypal core, which silently instructs the particular field of the various ways to contain. One archetype on which many of these containers are modeled is the *uroborus*, a universal motif of a serpent coiled into a circle, biting its own tail. As a symbol of infinite unity and unimagined wholeness, it is a primary metaphor for the earliest stage of human development in which there is no differentiation, no delineation, no individual consciousness. The uroborus appears as the round "container", the maternal womb, or anything big and embracing that contains, surrounds, enwraps, shelters, and nurtures something nascent. All these belong to this archetype. In relation to human development, the uroborus is not limited only to the symbol of a woman's womb, but also to a world or cosmic region where hidden contents have their essential abode. In *Origins and History of Consciousness* (1954), Neumann describes this aspect of the metaphor of the uroborus:

> This living image of the Great and Good Mother has at all times of distress been the refuge of humanity and ever

shall be; for the state of being contained in the whole,
without responsibility or effort, with no doubts and no
division of the world into two, is paradisal, and can never
again be realized in its pristine, happy-go-luckiness in adult
life. (p. 15)

Neumann goes on to describe the dual nature of the uroborus, both positive and negative. In its positive aspects, the uroborus protects the embryonic ego, much like the mother protects the infant as it gathers the necessary psychic apparatus to exist independently in the world. The positive uroboric state represents that phase in an individual's life where he/she relies on the holding qualities of the unconscious and the maternal environment. This begins in infancy, when the child is totally dependent on its environment for survival, and it is for this very reason that the quality of the maternal uroboric hold is vitally important. Neumann's maternal uroborus concept bears a striking resemblance to the physiological processes active during conception and pregnancy. The process whereby the fertilized egg bonds to the uterine lining may well be the archetypal dominant behind that stage where the nascent ego is contained within the uroborus. Without this initial bonding, the fetus cannot survive. Fetal attachment to the uterus represents the beginning phase of the child's dependence on the mother, while initiating its intrapsychic dependence on the maternal uroborus.

The destructive side of the uroborus is evidenced when the nascent ego struggles for independence, but then succumbs to the regressive pull of the unconscious, which works to undermine ego development and separation. As this tender ego is pulled back into the unconscious, it begins experiencing the uroboric hold as regressive, confining and annihilating. This regression is often referred to as uroboric incest. It is the desire to be dissolved and absorbed, the craving for unconsciousness, nostalgia and longing. When the ego passively melts back into the union with the Mother, it temporarily becomes equated with death and despair. Dream symbols that sometimes accompany this (often repeated) cycle of development often include caves, a sarcophagus, tombs or coffins. The regressive return to the Great Round is never the end, however, and the ego, after having been immersed in death, re-awakens to begin a new emergence.

Throughout the life process, an individual constantly struggles with these two aspects of the uroborus. Regressive pulls occur as the individual falters in his/her handling of reality. However, there are times when the individual needs temporarily to suspend ego-consciousness and return to the unconscious. For instance, after the completion of a project requiring great concentration from the ego, the return to the unconscious serves to refuel the personality by allowing the individual a respite from external reality and a time to reconnect with the creative aspects of the unconscious.

During the initial stages of treatment, the patient often experiences the uroborus in a non-differentiated way. Many patients unconsciously long for the security of the maternal uroboric hold, yet desperately fear (because of its incest/death aspect) immersion into it. Langs (1984) makes this point in the following:

> ...the secure frame situation creates a dangerous claustrum that mobilizes the patient's basic phobic-paranoid-schizoid anxieties. The patient unconsciously feels entrapped by the conditions of treatment and develops morbid fears of the claustrum either in terms of abandonment and annihilation through deprivation and starvation, and/or annihilation through violence on the part of the therapist. (p.7)

Patients' fear of the uroboric/secure frame experience is seen in their requests for and acceptance of a treatment setting where blatant breaks in the ideal frame exist. I have observed that patients' demand for compromised treatment environments are directly related to the severity of traumatic experiences occurring during the maternal uroboric phase. The degree to which they refuse the analyst's offer of a secure therapeutic setting is directly proportional to their early traumatic experiences with the uroboric mother. By this, I am referring to any major disturbance to the uroboric hold. Any life-threatening experience, such as the actual death of a parent or sibling, a serious illness of self, parents, or siblings, family violence or other severely dysfunctional family dynamics, all work to jeopardize the child's experience of the world as protective.

Many patients unconsciously sense that destroying the curative factors of the analysis will help them avoid facing the terrors of their early experiences. Their acceptance of questionable therapeutic settings represents a repetition compulsion, in that they again find themselves in a faulty maternal environment. In this situation, the patient is driven by his defenses and unconsciously convinces himself that everyone is like the frightening parent. If, however, the patient and therapist were to establish a satisfying therapeutic relationship, the patient would suddenly be opened to the experience of trust, love, and security. If this can be accomplished, the patient is able to experience the contrast between the understanding received from the analyst and the terror that was introjected from the relationship to the destructive parent.

When the analyst recognizes the patient's terror of a secure treatment, she or he needs to apply the secure frame concept with patience, wisdom and kindness. To introduce a treatment setting where the patient's defenses are very quickly analyzed and disrespected will inevitably cause chaos within the patient, often resulting in premature termination. Early in my career, I had many cases where I failed to be judicious in applying the features of the secure frame, and many patients decided not to continue therapy. Initially I thought these terminations were attributed to a dread of meaning and of the secure frame. To a large extent this may have been true, but one learns as a therapist to be extremely sensitive when approaching patients' traumas and fears. Defenses are created to protect what is vulnerable, and it is wise to realize that many patients have needed to construct defenses to protect their internal worlds from repeated trauma. However, the danger and paradox here is that the very way we defend ourselves inevitably creates another traumatic experience. To expect them to immobilize their defenses by suddenly introducing them to treatment through the implementation of a secure frame is often too much for the patient to bear. A strong, caring alliance between patient and therapist needs to be established before the patient can accept the analytic relationship. The relationship needs to be strong enough to hold the patient in the therapy during both its protective and terrifying aspects.

A positive experience of treatment will make the patient vulnerable to his or her more guarded feelings towards the analyst and, in turn, receptive to the curative aspects of the unconscious. In order to reach this stage, the patient will eventually have to sacrifice ego control and dominance. This process cannot be forced by the analyst, and optimally will occur as the patient realizes how resistant he or she is to the therapist's offer of understanding and of his or her own (patient's) need for security and love. For instance, many patients whose early experiences were marked by violence and severe emotional disturbances within the family develop a militant stand against the world. This aggressive personal stance emerges in response to the threatening aspects of their reality, and points to the degree to which they had to sector off their need for understanding in order to survive. They had to control their lives through a masterful exertion of ego strength as a means of avoiding the chaos and simultaneously the need for care, comfort and love residing within their psyches and in their external environment. In many instances, as ego control lessens, the creative aspects of the unconscious become activated, evidenced through dreams, images and affects, and work toward a resolution of the patient's disturbances. Transformation cannot occur while the ego maintains dominance over the personality. As the ego's grip loosens, the individual is cast back into the unconscious and is forced to recognize both its positive and terrifying aspects.

Once patients begin to acknowledge the traumatic emotions and experiences residing within them, terrifying aspects of the unconscious begin to surface. As frightening as this material may be, an encounter with it represents the first time the individual truly enters the world, in that he or she no longer has to fight off the unconscious for fear of recalling past and internal distress. Marie Louise von Franz (1970) writes:

> If you venture yourself into life, into reality instead of keeping outside so as to avoid suffering, you will find that the earth...is like a fertile field on which you can work and that life is also death; that if you give yourself to reality, you will be disillusioned and the end of it will be that you will meet death. If you accept your life you really in the deepest sense of the word, accept death.... (p. 161)

The ego now begins its heroic pursuit toward independence and separation from the unconscious. Although consciousness has developed, the ego is still frail and easily seduced back into the Great Mother. Neumann (1954) attributes this regression to the ego's fear of being overpowered by reality; hence the ego retreats in hopes of finding refuge from the hostile outer (and inner) world. Developmentally this stage is seen in children during the rapprochement-separation phase, where the child longs for, yet fears its (relative) autonomy. Repeated experiences of the protective aspects of treatment cause a lessening of resistances and repressive forces. This in turn releases unconscious material.

The re-activation of unconscious forces in the personality creates the potential for loss of ego structure. It is this return of the unconscious in treatment that represents the reappearance of the Great Mother/Son Lover stage of archetypal development. (Neumann is using the metaphor of Mother/Son as equivalent to the relationship between the unconscious and the developing ego. He is attempting to describe the plight of the ego during the early stages of its development. Neither he nor I is attempting to indicate that developmental differences between males and females are irrelevant. The importance of those differences needs a separate discussion, not relevant to this one.) Neumann (1954) describes the terrifying aspects of the Great Mother/Maternal Uroborus when stating: "Death, castration and dismemberment are all the dangers that characterize the youthful lover and his relationship to the Great Mother" (p. 58).

This description suggests why the lessening of ego control and the experience of internal distress is dreaded.

A patient often experiences the *"devouring death mother"* during moments in treatment when the therapist makes an appropriate intervention, or in some other way demonstrates genuine understanding of his or her process. It is common for a patient to respond to a successful intervention in the initial interview by suddenly recalling a significant childhood trauma. For instance, after a meaningful intervention, a patient remembered being locked in a car with his psychotic mother. Another patient recalled being locked in the kitchen with his psychotic mother, who turned on the gas oven, hoping to kill both herself and her children. A third patient responded with the memory of his mother lunging after his father with a knife. There are a number of possible meanings to these images. One may be that they represent the patient's unconscious perceptions of the replicative, non-therapeutic and perhaps even destructive elements of the so-called *"secure frame"*, that is, that despite the analyst's belief in the curative nature of this type of therapeutic frame, it may in fact be destructive. I have also thought the images could relate to a break in the secure frame or to a faulty intervention. However, with the presence of strong validating images prior to the emergence of these traumatic memories, there was strong likelihood that the material represented the patients' *"secure frame dread."* These patients expressed their deepest fears during moments when they unconsciously felt understood by the therapist. The frequency of images concerning locked spaces, I believe, corresponds to their unconscious perceptions that treatment was being secured, yet security for them has always been amalgamated with patterns of psychotic mothering and/or terrifying experiences, and was something to be feared and avoided.

Initially, patients appreciate the healthy and protective qualities of the therapeutic setting, but quickly begin to feel the terror that had been repressed. At such a moment, the patient is led back into the realm of the death mother to face early experiences of death and despair. This death anxiety is attributed to two primary causes:

1. The actual threat to the patient's, parents', or sibling's life or to their psychological well-being.

2. To re-experience traumatic events means that the resistance against these memories has lessened, ushering in the previously repressed material. This prior ego structure has now given way to an authentic, yet fragile, nascent ego. This type of transformative event is often experienced as a death for the old ego structure.

Jung's (1962) personal descent into the unconscious was coupled with psychotic anxieties and fears. After his separation from Freud, the material erupting from his unconscious threatened to dissolve the stability of his ego. Writing about these experiences he states:

> At times this [feeling of disorientation] became so strong that I suspected some psychic disturbance in myself...The inner urgency mounted until the terrible moment came when the voice said, "if you do not understand...you must shoot yourself. (pp. 173, 180)

From these experiences, Jung learned that meaning for one's life was to be found through a confrontation with and understanding of the unconscious. This encounter required a cessation of ego dominance, as evidenced by Jung's allowing himself to be guided by the Self. He understood however, that an encounter with the Self may bring a confrontation with one's own psychotic core. Neumann (1954) echoes these sentiments when he describes the Great Mother as *she who drives men mad and fascinates* (p. 60).

Interpretative Activity and the Anima

As the therapist interprets his patients' unconscious material, a bridge to the unconscious is built. The analyst leads his/her patient into the unconscious through his sensitive and thoughtful commentaries of the patient's unconscious thoughts and feelings. The anima is described as that which leads men to their feelings and to their unconscious; so too does the meaningful interpretation. In offering an interpretation, the analyst temporarily functions as the patient's anima, serving to model and instruct him/her in a way of living with and understanding the unconscious. The power of the analyst's interpretative activity is described by Strachey (1934):

> At the moment of interpretation the analyst is in fact deliberately evoking a quantity of the patient's id-energy while it is alive and actual and unambiguous...Such a moment must above all others put to the test his relations with his own unconscious impulses. (p. 377)

We can re-interpret Strachey's *"id-impulses"* to mean *"activated unconscious contents."* The analyst begins drawing the curtain away from the patient's illusions about reality, and introduces him to the hidden workings of the unconscious.

Interpretations in the initial interview inform the patient of the value placed by the analyst on unconscious processes. The patient implicitly understands that if analysis is to succeed, the unconscious must be brought into the work. Early interpretations serve to empower patients, for they learn that the guiding force in the analysis will be their own unconscious, whose voice the therapist will listen to throughout the analysis.

As the analyst attends to the conditions of treatment and to the manifestations of the Self in the initial interview, he is doing something similar to what the ancient Asklepiads did in their healing practice. Asklepiads exercised careful attention to the details of the healing site because they understood that healing represented an epiphanous event. As the priests waited outside the *abaton* (healing chamber) for the patient to present his dream, they must have felt the anticipation of an encounter with the divine, knowing that the dream and the cure came directly from God.

I believe that a similar attitude of reverence for the psyche is engendered as analysts work to provide patients with a treatment setting that facilitates a meeting with the Self. To attend to unconscious communication in the initial interview is an act of respect for the objective psyche, and this attitude of respect encourages the unconscious to guide the therapeutic process.

THRESHOLD

EXPERIENCES

CHAPTER 3

THE RELATIONSHIP BETWEEN MOTHER/INFANT INTERACTIONS AND THE ESTABLISHMENT OF THE ANALYTIC RELATIONSHIP

J ust as infants require a tremendous emotional commitment from parental figures, patients demand similar emotional attention from their analysts. Everyone has the need for stability, consistency, and devotion to ensure successful development. A failure in any one of these areas will have important implications for a child's eventual physical and mental health, just as it would for the outcome of psychotherapy.

D.W. Winnicott, a pediatrician turned psychoanalyst and a member of the British school of Object Relations theorists who wrote prolifically about his study of mother/infant interactions, states in *The Theory of the Parent/ Infant Relationship* (1960):

> *The mental health of an individual...is laid down by this maternal care, which when it goes well, is scarcely noticed, and is a continuation of the physiological provision that characterizes the prenatal state. This environmental provision is also a continuation of the tissue aliveness and the functional health which (for the infant) provides silent but vitally important ego support. (p. 49)*

The child's need for a positive maternal bond has been proven empirically by Spitz's work (1945) with institutionalized children and Harlow's work (1962) with infant monkeys. Spitz observed that children under institutional care (as a result of the absence of the biological mother) developed severe emotional and physical disorders and, in some cases, died. Likewise, when Harlow separated infant monkeys from their mothers at birth, and a surrogate cloth mother was offered instead, he discovered that these infant monkeys failed to establish normal developmental patterns as adults. When the females became mothers, they failed to provide security or nurturance to their infants, and at times were even dangerous to their young.

A longitudinal study conducted by Beres and Obers (1950) examined the effects of severe maternal deprivation in children and its manifestation in adult life. Of the thirty-eight children followed during this study, four became psychotic, twenty-one had character disorders, and four were discovered to have other forms of mental illness. Only seven percent were found to have made a satisfactory adult development.

Maternal devotion is evidenced in many ways: a mother's facial expression as she holds her infant, the way she carefully tests the temperature of the baby's food, and the various activities she shares with the child.[1] Winnicott (1964) portrays this level of maternal devotion in his description of his observations of mothers feeding their infants:

> When I see in what a delicate way a mother who is not anxious manages the situation, I am always astounded. You see her there, making the baby comfortable and arranging a setting in which the feeding may happen. If all goes well, the setting is part of the human relationship. (p. 89)

The emotional and physical setting created by the mother conveys her love and concern for her child's welfare. Each of the authors cited in this chapter point to the essential need of the infant to experience security, protection, and love, and stress how the absence of this maternal "holding" causes severe disturbances in the child's development and maturation.

Much of what has been learned about mother-infant interaction has important implications for the formation of the therapeutic relationship. Much like the infant's need for security in the womb, patients too require a secure and protective setting within which to carry out their analytic work. Winnicott (1964) discusses the parallels between therapeutic work and the mother-child relationship when he advises therapists that "...[their] function can logically be viewed in terms of infant care, that is in terms of the facilitating environment, the facilitation of the maturational processes" (p. 98).

Michael Fordham (1976), a Jungian analyst with extensive experience with children, arrived at a similar understanding of the clinical situation:

The approach I have come to consider most valuable is a mixture of analysis and special care. By special care, I shall mean that the therapist aims to meet and respond to the child at a very early level of development and so provides conditions for the self to grow and develop. To do so, he is required to rely on his own feelings, just as the mother responds empathically to the cues provided by her infant in such a way that the child's own sense of self may be recognized and grow. (p. 139)

The treatment suggested by Winnicott and Fordham is important for understanding the patient's experience of the initial interview. Just as children are affected by both the mother's moods and ways of interacting, so too, are patients in the initial interview sensitive to the mood and ways of interacting of the analyst. The children will respond to the conditions of what Winnicott calls *the maternal hold*, and will represent their experience of it through their actions. Much of the children's behavior represents an introjection of their perceptions of the attitudes expressed towards them. For instance, a child who has been the object of contempt will grow up to feel self-contempt. As this child develops, he or she begins feeling that there are objective reasons for self-hatred, such as being too fat, too thin, or not smart enough. However, the child fails to understand that these feelings were instilled by the actions and attitudes of a parental figure. It is almost inevitable that a parent will at some point commit what Kohut termed an *empathic failure,* which can range from minor to monumental. In the worst extreme it is the kind of active trauma that crosses boundaries and is experienced as violent (physical, emotional or sexual). In the lesser version, empathic failure is a form of neglect-not being on time with feedings, not keeping the baby warm enough, not holding, or not noticing what the child needs. In either case, empathic failure results in a pathological fusion in which the boundaries between the "offender" and the "victim" are dis-regulated and re-drawn. At the very moment of danger, in order to maintain the relationship with the parent, the child will take in the shame the parent should feel, will contort him or herself into whatever shape the parent needs, and will assume the perspective of the perpetrator in order to maintain the connection. This willingness to unconsciously identify with the parent is one of the most powerful and pervasive forces in human development. It is the way trauma manifests as sadness and terror, and the way the child begins to develop shame as a core of its identity. To be healed, the patient will have to discover where these feelings originated and, especially, realize that these feelings (of anger, disdain or neglect) were, in fact, directed at him/her.

This interpersonal/intrapsychic/interactional developmental schema originates at birth (although some analysts suggest that the fetus records experiences from the moment of conception), when the child is forced to adapt to the emotional elements of its world. Whether the child experiences maternal deprivation, neglect, threats of annihilation, or the experience of being loved, he or she child will introject these feelings and respond accordingly.

Drawing on findings from mother-infant interactions, various clinicians have attempted to establish a secure and protective environment in the therapeutic relationship. Langs's "secure frame theory" recommends a therapeutic setting which, in many respects, offers qualities of the original dyadic womb experience and the experience of a newborn who is lucky enough to be tended by what Winnicott termed "a good enough mother"—who tries her best to duplicate the womb experience after birth by providing a protective envelope of care in which the child is kept at the right temperature, clean, held, appropriately fed, and given enough time to rest. The secure frame in psychotherapy consists of the analyst's offer of a treatment setting where the following ground rules are practiced: set time, set fee, total confidentiality, anonymity of the therapist, and the use of appropriate silence and interpretive interventions. These are all geared toward offering the patient a protective, private, and uncontaminated setting. This establishes a "therapeutic hold" that is analogous to the "maternal hold." Both demand a kind of steady preoccupation with the quality of the relationship. Langs advocates the application of this set of ground rules because, he claims, patients invariably request these conditions unconsciously.

Just as patients and children respond to the positive aspects of the protective maternal hold, they also react to its disruption. Disturbances in healthy functioning are usually an indication of a breakdown of the maternal hold. With the analytic patient (adult or child), disturbances often emerge at times of stress and anxiety. However, when this happens, it is important to examine the quality of the therapeutic hold, and to see if there is a correlation between the emergence of the patient's symptoms and a breakdown in the holding qualities of the analytic relationship. It can be assumed that patients respond to their unconscious awareness of breaks in analytic security through an activation of their symptoms. One study that attempted to correlate the relationship between patients' disturbances and the quality of treatment was conducted by Morgan (1983) who writes:

> [The] so-called iatrogenic disease is often an unconscious collusion between doctor and patient, resulting in a matrix of miscommunications in which the smoothness of the

transaction between the two is disrupted, resulting in
damage to the patient and also to the doctor. (p. 148)

Faulty interventions and breaks in the frame are experienced by the patient as non-holding and destructive.[2] Inappropriate interventions imply that the therapist's distress has become mobilized and that she or he is unable to metabolize her or his own internal conflicts. These disturbances force a shift of attention from the patient to the therapist. As a result, the therapist's unconscious disturbances come to occupy center stage in the analysis.[3] When this happens, the secure hold is temporarily broken, and the patient is forced to emotionally retreat from the analytic process until the disruption is discussed and resolved.

Patients may respond to the implication of breaks in analytic security through derivative communication and unconscious behavior. They will use whatever method of adaptation they have developed in the past to handle empathic failures. Winnicott (1960) discusses the effect on patients of the breakdown of the maternal hold: "The alternative to being is reacting, and reacting interrupts being....The holding environment therefore has as its main function the reduction to a minimum of impingements to which the infant must react..." (p. 47).

Patients often defend themselves against the recognition of faulty interventions and mismanagements of the therapeutic environment by merging with and introjecting the poorly functioning therapist. This is clinically evidenced in cases where the therapist disrupts the analytic setting. The patient may exhibit regressive behavior. Neurotic symptoms may reappear. Similar to the infant's inability to metabolize its feelings about the loss of the maternal hold, patients protect themselves from conscious recognition that their security (in treatment) is temporarily lost. In these instances, the activation of the patients' regressive behavior often represents a primitive defense for handling traumas incurred with the breakdown of analytic security. Melanie Klein (1961) spent much of her analytic career studying children's responses to their maternal environment. She discovered that children often unconsciously incorporate the defective/pathogenic parent in an effort to avoid realizing the harmful qualities of the relationship. She presents the following brief clinical example to illustrate her understanding of incorporation: "When mommy had a headache or felt sick, the child often said that it was his fault, because he had been naughty" (p. 79).

In the initial interview, patients often unconsciously respond to breaks in the secure frame through the utilization of incorporative defenses. For example, a female clinic patient began the initial session by describing feelings of being unwanted and undesirable. As the session progressed, she revealed that she had waited more than four months for her first appointment, and during this time there had been a breakdown in her communications with the clinic staff. As we discussed this, it became clear that her feelings of being unwanted were directly related to her unconscious experience with the clinic.

Neumann's (1954) description of the uroborus offers an important archetypal perspective from which to understand the meaning of the maternal hold:

> *Enfolded and upborne by great Mother Nature, rocked in her arms, he is delivered over to her for good or evil. Nothing is himself; everything is world. The world shelters and nourishes him, while he scarcely wills or acts at all. (p. 15)*

His portrayal of the maternal uroborus is strikingly similar to Winnicott's "maternal hold", to Langs's "secure frame", and Jung's "analytical (alchemical) container". The following diagrams represent uroboric states of successful/empathic responses and negative uroboric experiences for the child:

Diagram A: Secure Maternal Hold

Uroboric Container
Environment Created by Mother

Maternal Successful/
Sympathetic Response to Child

*Creates relative calm and security for
the child in the maternal environment.*

Child / Ego

Diagram B: Breakdown of Secure Hold

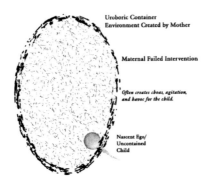

Uroboric Container
Environment Created by Mother

Maternal Failed Intervention

*Often creates chaos, agitation,
and havoc for the child.*

Nascent Ego/
Uncontained
Child

The diagrams portray both the child's and the patient's reliance on the maternal/therapeutic environment.

Diagram A - represents the mother's attunement to the child. Here the child's needs are sensitively met by the attending mother. The child experiences the mother as a self-object who satisfies its needs and exists solely to attend to its care. The child is protected and secure in this setting, feeling that the mother's involvement is a product of her love for him. This positive uroboric experience is described by Alice Miller (1981), who writes:

If a child is lucky enough to grow up with a mirroring mother who allows herself to be cathected narcissistically, who is at the child's disposal-that is, the mother who allows herself to be made use of as a function of the child's narcissistic development, then a healthy self feeling can gradually develop in the growing child. (p. 32)

Diagram B - shows the mother's utilization of the child as a narcissistic object. Her interventions and attempts at childcare represent a refusal or inability to acknowledge the child's needs. This child does not exist as a separate entity from the mother. In time the child will have to acknowledge that its function was to play a supportive role to the mother's ego, and that the child's genuine needs and existence have never been attended to or validated. This is in fact a death experience for the child, in that the mother's disinterest in the child becomes translated as her unconscious wish that her child's autonomy will perish and that he or she will remain eternally by the mother's side. Miller (1981) proceeds to describe this destructive mother/infant relationship:

Quite unconsciously and despite her own good intentions, the mother then tries to assuage her own narcissistic needs through her child, that is, she cathects him narcissistically.... Instead, he develops something the mother needs...(which may prevent him, throughout his life, from being himself). (pp. 34 -35)

The therapeutic setting serves as a stimulus to which the patient unconsciously responds. Thus, the unconscious matrix of each intervention and condition of treatment needs to be understood. However, therapists' reliance on transference theory has clouded the importance of the bi-personal therapeutic field.[4] For instance, the patient responds to a specific intervention by presenting derivative material rich in stories about seduction. The therapist tends to assign a transference interpretation to this response. However, the process of ascribing patients' responses to transference (past-oriented) and fantasy often serves the purpose of preserving the therapist's integrity, which, in effect, denies the patient's objective experience in treatment.

Additionally, such consciously-derived communication lacks the derivative depth found in unconscious, objectively valid communication.

This trend of viewing patients' material as distortion, fantasy and projection (untruths) began with Freud's rejection of the seduction theory. Initially, Freud believed the stories he heard in therapy of parental abuse and misconduct, but quickly retracted his opinion and began writing that these stories were products of the imagination. Fortunately, Masson (1984), who had been curator of the Freud archives, studied the unconscious motives for Freud's abandonment of the seduction theory, and the implications that this had for psychotherapeutic treatment.

> *...Freud had decided that the seductions had never occurred, that the parents had not done anything to their children in reality.... An act was replaced by an impulse, a deed by a fantasy. This new "reality" came to be so important for Freud that the impulses of parents against their children were forgotten, never to reclaim importance in his writings. (p. 59)*

Masson (1984) states that Freud abandoned the seduction theory, not for theoretical or clinical reasons, but for "complex personal ones" (p. 59). Masson's work helps us to gain a clearer understanding of the mother-child relationship as well as of the initial interview situation. It represents an attempt to revalidate children's and patients' objective experiences.

The examination of Freud's rejection of the seduction theory may provide insight into ways in which individuals and therapists create illusions and theories to defend against recognizing internal distress. To reject the idea of child abuse serves to protect ourselves against the terror of our own conscious, and especially, unconscious intentions. The parent or adult who sexually abuses the child is, in effect, killing its victim. Such a person has no concern for the child's welfare, only for his or her own gratification. But the child and the perpetrator of the crime need to face the truth and meaning of their actions. The victim must realize that this person tried to kill him/her, and the abusive adult (in order to heal) must realize that he or she actively threatened the child's life.

Parents' behavior toward their children is usually based on good intentions, but these too can be injurious. The same is true with analytic work, in that the entire field of psychotherapy and psychoanalysis is still in its infancy. Unfortunately, analysts fail to recognize that they do have the benefit of objective methods of validation, like those that help guide physicians in their work with patients (such as blood tests, x-rays, etc.). While dreams and derivatives do offer objectively valid means of assessment, these are often overlooked in treatment. In turn we find that a great deal of analytic practice is still good wishes, speculation, and a sincere desire to help.

Much of what we do with patients is based on conjecture, usually influenced by our personal beliefs and prejudices. As a result our conclusions need to be seen as speculative at best. By examining mother-infant interactions through direct observation, we can discern what the child experiences as helpful and nurturing. Likewise, by carefully analyzing the behaviors and unconscious communications within the analytic framework, we can observe how patients unconsciously respond to the conditions of treatment and analytic interactions.

CHAPTER 4

THE RELATIONSHIP BETWEEN JUNG'S ASSOCIATION TEST, THE THEORY OF THE COMPLEX, AND THE DERIVATIVE

From experiences and observations while working in the Burgholzli Hospital in Zurich, Jung realized that powerful unseen forces were responsible for his patients' behaviors. While the prevailing methods of treatment at that time had little if anything to do with the uncovering of unconscious dynamics, Jung turned his brilliant lens to the workings of the psyche and its effects on the personality. In time, he developed the Association Test as a way to access the dynamics of the unconscious, and better understand the interactions between ego-consciousness and the contrapuntal influence of unconscious processes.

The Association Test is a list of about a hundred words. The test person is instructed to react with the first (one) word that comes into his or her mind as quickly as possible after the presentation of the stimulus word. The person's reaction time is marked by a stop-watch. After completing the test, the same procedure is repeated and the individual is instructed to reproduce his previous answers. In certain places memory fails and "mistakes" appear. The mistakes are important because they provide evidence of psychological activity that Jung (following the work of Pierre Janet) called a *complex*. The Association Test is the precursor to what is now known as a lie detector test. Both document that the energy force generated by the mobilization of unconscious contents (complexes) significantly interferes with the ego's ability to reproduce the previous response.

In constructing the Association Test, Jung discovered that when he presented a patient a list of selected words (some of which are very benign like chair and others more controversial like father or mother) and asked them to respond verbally, some responses were immediate and others took longer. The longer it took to get a response, the greater it was assumed was the power of the complex. In addition to recording the patient's response time, Jung's protocol also noted when the patient showed physiological responses to the stimulus words such as sweating, fidgeting, or change of facial expression.[1]

Words that produced the greatest number of "mistakes" were seen as indices of unconscious activity. The stimulus words were understood to activate the patient's complex, which Jung defined as an unconscious conglomeration of psychic contents characterized by a peculiar or perhaps painful feeling tone, hidden from the patient's awareness. When activated, a complex disrupts usual modes of functioning and acts like a mini-ego, which he sometimes called a "splinter self" that created maladaptive behaviors and disproportional bursts of affect.[2]

A goal of the Association Test (and Jungian analysis) is to bring the patient into a conscious awareness of the unconscious content and to understand its meaning. This movement of energy from the unconscious to consciousness changes the patient's psychological balance by freeing energy from the complex and making it accessible for conscious, adaptive use. As the complex loses intensity, the ego gains greater responsibility. Without consciousness, our capacity to choose and to act with morality and integrity is severely limited.

In *Analytical Psychology: Its Theory and Practice* (1968), Jung described the procedure of giving the Association Test to a thirty-five year old man. He observed that the following words received a delayed response: knife, lance (spear), to beat, pointed, and bottle. Weaving together the narrative of these words, Jung reported the following sequence.

> He said to the man "I did not know you had had such a disagreeable experience." The man stared at Jung and said, "I don't know what you're talking about". Jung said, "You know you were drunk and had a disagreeable affair sticking your knife into somebody". (p. 56)

The test subject then confessed to his part in the whole event.[3] Subsequent to such results, Jung's Association Test became recognized as being so successful at bringing previously unconscious information into consciousness that Jung was asked to use it with suspected Swiss criminals. The test was eventually refined and developed into what is now known as the modern day "lie detector test".

What Jung demonstrated in these tests (among many other things) is that a word, like the dream image, can spontaneously and accurately evoke an entire story. The word "shark" for instance brings a whole visual drama to life—predatory, dangerous, a fish in the deep sea, with bad eyesight, a heightened sense of smell, and a deadly result if antagonized or aroused. The word shark itself can be understood simply as a manifest communication from the ego or it can be understood as an archetypal symbol. The task of the analyst is to determine the word's latent, objective archetypal meaning—a symbol chosen by the objective psyche to represent an archetypal, *a priori* experience of human response.[4]

Jung's brilliant theoretical discoveries from the empirical responses to the Association Test led him to a greater understanding of the power of the complex. Eventually he referred to complexes as the *via regia* (or royal road) to the unconscious, and as "the architect of dreams."

Jung recognized that the careful analysis of a patient's words and patterns of communication leads directly to both the personal unconscious and to the dominant archetypal patterns of the objective psyche.iv The findings from the Association

Test provided strong empirical evidence about the structure of the psyche, how a patient's language directly relates to unconscious processes within his or her psyche, and the evocative precision contained within the human language.

The presence of a sudden, unusually strong emotional affect in the patient, obvious behavioral disturbances and/or ego-dystonic prejudices or attitudes are all indications that a complex has been constellated (or activated). After recognizing the emotional activation of a complex, the initial therapeutic task is to determine which complex is activated, to understand the immediate stimulus that triggered its emergence, and to integrate the archetypal aspects of the complex into the personality.

If we imagine how a patient reacts to the word "power" we could infer a complex has been activated if he or she responds with the word "abuse" because power in and of itself is not necessarily about abuse. The patient's "complexed" reaction signals an accurate representation of his or her personal experience with power and a troubled relationship to the archetypal issue of power.

Power in a universal sense, is defined as "the ability to do or act, capability of doing or effecting something, a particular faculty of body or mind" (Barnhart and Stein, Eds.,1963, p. 950).[5]

Power exists in the pantheon of archetypes of the human psyche as one of many elemental energies that drive individual and collective experience. While a patient may have had terrible experiences with the abuse and misuse of power, the archetype of power itself remains as a stable configuration within the objective psyche. One's personal experience will not affect the archetype, but it does affect an individual's capacity to apprehend its objective meaning. For example, knowing that a dip in the pool on a hot summer day could be refreshing is an objective reality. Being unable to avail oneself of a refreshing dip because a family member had died in the pool is an example of how subjective experience can create a complex that interferes with clear objective understanding. In this regard we can see the relationship between the personal complex and the archetypal backdrop from which it springs. "Power" is not inherently abusive just as swimming pools are not inherently dangerous. But in the case of the complexed response, the personal experience of the patient distorts the objective reality and becomes the only lens from which he or she can apprehend the archetypal. The individual "lens" of the complex always distorts and limits our capacity to see the objective truth of the archetype.

The following clinical vignette illustrates a number of central points about the complex. A patient I had been seeing for a number of months arrived at her session saying that she had a disturbing thought while driving. She imagined that God was pulling plants, shrubs and other things growing in the ground, out by their roots. She talked about seeing a man stabbed on the street, with blood rushing out of a wide gash, and images about a space shuttle disaster. In addition to the human tragedy incurred by the shuttle event, she was also affected by the fact that the shuttle exploded so soon after take off.

Our discussion of the violent stories and images of things being prematurely terminated or torn out by the roots eventually revealed the unconscious dynamics of a recent abortion. The image of the uprooted shrubs may be seen as the Self's actual experience of the psychological effects of the event, and also as a clear and accurate description of the biological facts of abortion in which a living fetus is actually uprooted. In working with this material I attempted to help the patient identify with her personal and archetypal experiences of this event, and hoped to help her separate from its collective cultural and religious overtones, so that we could work with the deepest aspects of the abortion experience. Because abortion refers to the decision to terminate something that is alive and growing, we needed to see if there were other areas where a new life or initiative was prematurely ended. The complex she presented centered around a dominant theme of premature termination.

As the unconscious revealed the troubling aspects of the abortion, it was obvious that its significance in her life needed to be explored. However, because of the intense power of this image and her experience, I felt an additional question had to be asked regarding the sudden appearance of the unconscious material in the analysis. I needed to ask: *"Why is this material being presented now, and why has this event occurred at this particular point in the treatment?"*

In understanding the role of the unconscious to explicate interactional as well as intrapersonal dynamics, I had to wonder if the occurrence of the abortion also revealed something significant about the therapeutic relationship. While traditional therapeutic practice generally looks at client material as commentaries about intrapsychic concerns and distress, this position needs to be amended to include the possibility that these images and stories are also commentary on the current interpersonal aspects of the analysis.

An examination of the derivative meaning did in fact reveal a serious intrusion of a third party into the treatment relationship. At the time of the patient's abortion, the therapist's parents described an event where they had met a lovely woman from New York in the town where they had a vacation home. They had mentioned their son was in the "psychology field" and "this woman" expressed interest in meeting him. Immediately, the therapist sensed the stirrings of something odd, and discouraged his parents from ever mentioning his name or even saying their surname to her. Upon further questioning it became obvious to the therapist that the woman his parents had met was indeed his client. While important as a synchronistic event, its meaning was never fully understood. However we can see how the abortion images also now revealed her unconscious awareness of this intrusion into the treatment. While this event in and of itself was a break in the secure frame of the analytic boundaries, its potential to escalate could have caused a deeply wounding or fatal blow to the analysis. In this regard, the "chance" meeting between the therapist's parents and his client did in fact threaten the security of treatment. If the therapist's parents had persisted in their hope to arrange a meeting between them, the secure therapeutic container most probably would have been aborted.

The next illustration again captures the tendency of a constellated complex to draw both patient and therapist into a mutual field of influence.[6] This is the case of a woman being seen in a low cost treatment center staffed by analysts in training. The majority of sessions were often interrupted by the sounds of laughter and other loud noises erupting from adjacent therapy rooms. Although the patient's conscious reaction was to simply avoid and overlook the noise, her dreams and other derivative communications indicated a tremendous unconscious sensitivity to the disruptive quality of the situation. One day when the noise was excessive, she related the following story:

> *We were rehearsing for the play the other day and had just reached the most important moment, when suddenly these workmen came barging into the room. The rehearsal had to be stopped, everything was ruined at this point; the moment was lost. This had happened a number of times before, but I just learned to live with it. Now, I realize we have to find another place to rehearse where we will be assured privacy and protection from intrusions.*

This story clearly reveals her unconscious reaction to the noise, and we can see that her unconscious offered a meaningful solution-to find a private space to rehearse, which is translated as the need to find a private space for treatment. While the above is relatively easy to understand, this therapeutic "disruption" revealed pivotal information about a central complex in her life. In this regard, the therapeutic setting provided the stimulus for the emergence of a complex in much the same way the words in the association test served to elicit a response.

This patient, Pamela, was repeatedly involved with destructive men, none of whom could provide any semblance of security or sense of trust. Through the analysis it was clear that these relationships were modeled after her primary attachment with a borderline mother and absentee father. Her core issue centers on the unreliable and destructive mother complex, which in this case is extended to include the entire maternal field she experienced in childhood, including not only the mother, but also the loss of the father.

I worked to help her understand that treatment now echoed many of the more pernicious aspects of her past, and my inability to provide her with a greater sense of security and/or privacy brought me into her life as another faltering figure. However, Pamela was reluctant to make this connection, preferring to see me (consciously) as a helpful and benevolent figure. Her reaction is understandable, especially in light of Melanie Klein's description of the *narcissistic defense*, which poignantly captures a child's terror to see his or her central caretaker as flawed. Klein explains that to do so could seriously threaten a child's sense of security and in defense against this realization, the child becomes a scapegoat, unconsciously preferring to see him or herself as faulty and bad. These behaviors tend to remain in force throughout adult life, making it all the more difficult for clients to see the shortcomings and faults of other significant figures in their life.

The stories about disruptions in the theater and the desire for a private space were presented to show her deep need for protection. The therapist suggested that continuing treatment at the clinic may no longer be workable and suggested that treatment be moved to the therapist's private office, away from the clinic. While this transition would evoke both a positive and perhaps even a frightening response, it did represent a meaningful alternative to their current situation.

The objective psyche constantly produces derivative communications both about the patient's inner world and his or her response to the analytic experience. The derivative communication offers the most detailed and accurate presentation of the individual's unconscious perceptions of the multi-layered analytical situation.

When patients arrive in treatment and describe the reasons that brought them to the therapist's office, they generally believe that the reason for discussing the particular disturbing incident or circumstances is to convey the impact of their experience to the therapist. While this initial level of information sharing is critically important in order to understand the manifest concerns of the patient, it is only one dimension (and intention) of a powerful, complex interactive system of human communication.

Treatment that is maintained at the level of manifest communication fails to understand the patient's unconscious experiences because it denies access to the deeper reaches of the patient's psyche. For that reason I believe it is critical to the success of the analysis to convey to patients the importance of derivative communication. It is in this way that access to the complex and to the workings of the psyche can be mined and understood.

Because derivative communication bypasses ego functioning, it represents an unbiased and accurate perception of the patient's self. Just as the dream and the appearance of archetypal material reveal truths about the patient's life, so too does the derivative communication connect the patient to the authentic meaning of his or her unconscious experience of the analytic work. The derivative material activates and liberates the emotional potential of the complex to override the patient's ego defensive patterns. The analyst's interpretation of the situation then allows the patient to transform unconscious energy into meaning and conscious adaptation.

Jung understood the limited value of exploring patients' conscious responses during the Association Test. To discover the presence and meaning of a complex, Jung warned that:

If you asked directly about the strongest disturbances, you would get wrong answers, so...first ask the test person about the words which are not going directly to the kernel...you begin with relatively harmless works and you are likely to get an honest reply. (1968)

He described the patient's resistance to facing the truth of a particular situation and suggested that a way to meaning is found by taking an indirect route, one that circumvents ego functioning, which is exactly the way derivative communications function.

When one is trained in the art of understanding unconscious communication, it is difficult not to be impressed with the validity of unconscious, derivative perceptions, which in Jungian parlance equates to communications from the Self. A brief example will illustrate this level of psychic functioning of the derivative.

The clinical situation involves my accepting a referral from a current patient, Sarah. It so happened that at the time, I was studying the effects of patient referrals on both the patient being referred and the patient making the referral. The data I accumulated suggested a correspondence between the current patient's feelings of loss and lack of protection within the analysis when the newer patient began analysis. I had accepted this referral for a number of reasons, one of which was to earn a living, and also because I wanted to learn more about the impact of the boundary issues involved in cross-referrals.

The referred patient, Paul, twenty-two years old, entered the office and began discussing the following:

My problem is that I can't seem to stick to what I believe in. I'm often in situations where I've done all this studying, like on tests in school, and have come up with some conclusive results, but at the crucial moment, I'm unable to stand up for my beliefs. I've had this problem for years and if I don't get a handle on it, I'm going to really hurt myself.

These communications paralleled my own feelings about having accepted the consultation. Inwardly, I had already arrived at a relatively clear understanding of the issue of patient referrals, but failed to bring my beliefs into practice.

The following session with Sarah (after my consultation with Paul) produced equally startling material. Sarah arrived fifteen minutes late for the appointment. She wondered how the interview with Paul had gone. Then she explained that she was late because she stopped to answer the phone as she was leaving the house.

> *"I knew it would be a mistake to answer the call, but felt I just had to do it," she said. She continued, "Sometimes I feel compelled to do things I know aren't good for me."*

Then she mentioned that her husband had just joined a class that she was attending, and ever since his participation, she had lost interest in it.

This material can be heard as her unconscious perceptions that I should not have accepted Paul's request for treatment, and that I was doing something that was not good for her, Paul, or myself. The story about the husband joining her class, and her loss of interest can be understood as her feelings that Paul had joined her class (the analysis), and that now my attention would be shifted to him instead of to her. Unconsciously, she had experienced the situation as my having lost interest in her, and to a large extent this was her unconscious motivation for making the referral, as she desperately feared security.

This patient had grown up with a schizophrenic father whose lack of attentiveness resulted in the death of the patient's younger brother.[7] The patient was afraid to be alone with me because in her mind, to some extent I had become like the father (psychotic), failed to care for her, and could even cause her death. There were many other feelings about the psychotic father that she tried to avoid.[8] As a result of the material from these sessions, I discussed with Paul his need for a private therapeutic experience, where he would not have to share the therapist with a friend. (I did not confirm that I knew the third party.) I suggested that he think about this and get back to me. Within a few days, the patient called to say that he appreciated our discussion and would find another therapist. Subsequently I discussed with Sarah her derivatives regarding perceptions and experience of me and the therapy in light of my accepting the referral. This opened an entire area into her younger brother's death that had never been examined before.

The issues presented by both patients were grounded in complexes that needed to be understood. However, this material also referred to a personal complex I had been affected by at the time of this incident. Our psyches were intertwined at this point, and if the issues had not been rectified and understood, the situation would certainly have spiraled into more convoluted relational dynamics. Their derivative communications and images operated far beyond the capabilities of ordinary ego functioning and implied the intelligence that exists within the unconscious. This level could be considered a dimension of human experience that Jung termed *psychoid*—a reality in which he indicated that psyche and matter are two aspects of the same thing, and that communication between the two realms may be co-incidental in ways rational comprehension cannot explain. As such, the derivative communications of the two patients described above were uncannily, accurately attuned to my inner feelings, which at that time were still partially unconscious and may have been representative of the realm of connection that Jung had described as psychoidal.

Mindell (1973) discusses the psychoidal dimension of psyche and the transference and describes psychoidal as: "An adjective to describe a lower, deeper understanding of the image, where it is partly physical and partly psychological (p. 15)."

He describes psychoidal functioning in the transference to mirror the *"irreversible coupled phenomena"* in physics. Mindell describes four types of *"coupled psychoidal processes"*:

1. *matter-matter couplings* – such as a woman who feels a great throb in her body at the moment her sister is dying from cancer in the same organ.

2. *matter-psyche couplings* – such as dreams of other people or events of which we have as yet no conscious knowledge

3. *psyche-matter couplings* – such as psychosomatic illnesses

4. *psyche-psyche couplings* – such as transference phenomena, or dreams which reveal not the physical condition, but rather the unconscious or intimate affairs of someone else about whom we have no conscious knowledge.

These illustrations of patients, who unconsciously presented accurate, objective representations of the therapist's internal dynamics, fall into the psyche-to-psyche coupling. Such examples of derivative communication suggest the presence of an intimate, generative relationship between the empirical ego and its trans-conscious foundation that Jung called the Self.[9]

CHAPTER 5

JUNG'S INITIAL INTERVIEW

I t is difficult to gain a clear picture of Jung's clinical approach. His recorded case studies demonstrate that he followed no exact procedure nor behaved in exactly the same way with his patients.[1] In *Jung: Man and Myth*, Brome (1978) an historian of psychoanalytic and analytical psychology writes:

> *Jung had by now developed his therapeutic practice as well as theory in contrast to Freud's.... Jung's [patients] did not lie on the couch, but sat in a chair and the length and frequency of sessions varied.... [Jung] might sit looking out on the lake with the patient in any position he or she pleased. Sometimes he even treated patients on board his boat and on one occasion went careening around the lake in a high wind, singing, as part of the therapy. (p. 177)*

This portrait of Jung shows the idiosyncratic nature of his work, his high regard for individual expression, and his opposition to the Freudian ethos. Jung's clinical style may have developed as a mixture of his own unique personality and in reaction to Freud's seeming rigidity.

Brome (1978) discusses Jung's consultation with Sir Montague Norman, then "governor of the Bank of England." He consulted Jung on the advice of a friend after suffering an eczema attack. In the initial interview, Jung ordered a blood and spinal test for his patient. By the second interview, Jung arrived at the following diagnosis: "Norman was suffering from general paralysis of the insane, an incurable by-product of syphilis, telltale signs of which were the delusions of grandeur...unmistakably betrayed by the patient" (pp. 182 - 183).

Needless to say, the patient was "shattered" by Jung's interpretation, but decided to continue treatment.

Brome is quick to point out that at the time of the interview with Mr. Norman, Jung (following the break in his relationship with Freud) was beginning his own emotional breakdown.[2] Jung's interpretation indicates that he may have been unconsciously projecting his own emotional turmoil onto the patient.

A second report of Jung's work in the initial consultation is found in *Structure and Dynamics of the Psyche* (1960, ¶ 478). In the first session, the patient presented the following dream:

I dreamt that I was in a bare room. A sort of nurse received me, and wanted me to sit at a table on which stood a bottle of fermented milk, which I was supposed to drink. I wanted to go to Dr. Jung, but the nurse told me that I was in a hospital and that Dr. Jung had no time to receive me. (p. 249)

The associations were recorded as follows:

Bare Room: A sort of frosty reception room, as in an official building, or the waiting room of a hospital. I was never in a hospital as a patient.

Nurse: She looked repulsive; she was cross-eyed. That reminds me of a fortune teller and palmist whom I once visited to have my fortune told. Once I was sick and had a deaconess as a nurse.

Bottle of Fermented Milk: Nauseating. I cannot drink it. My wife is always drinking it, and I make fun of her for this because she is obsessed with the idea that one must always be doing something for one's health. I remember I once was in a sanitarium-my nerves were not so good and there I had to drink fermented milk.(p. 249)

The patient later admitted to once having been in a mental hospital and that his problems were still not resolved. His wife had been urging him to see Jung because of the reappearance of his problems.

Jung interpreted the dream, saying that the patient has to swallow a bitter drink (his problem) and that he unconsciously consulted Jung not as an analyst but as a fortune teller, who would magically relieve him of the problems.

Today, from a perspective enhanced by more than a half century of psychoanalytic scholarship, new questions arise about Jung's interpretation of this case. Jung viewed the dream as the patient's unconscious reactions to beginning treatment. This can be seen as one aspect of the dream's meaning, but other factors may need to be considered to understand the more far reaching aspects of the dream.

A first question to ask about the dream is why would the patient's decision to begin treatment be represented as coming to a bare room? On one hand, the image could be a compensation for the patient's reluctance to recognize his own psychological disturbances, his emotional barrenness and sterility. On the other hand, the dream could reflect the patient's unconscious perceptions of what he expected or was receiving from Jung and the prospects of beginning analytic treatment. Whether or not the dreamer was familiar with the concept of the analyst attempting to be a "blank slate" as recommended by some of the psychoanalytic practitioners at the time is unknown. If he had been familiar with that concept, it may have influenced the dream imagery.

The next dream image is of the nurse who receives the patient prior to the appointment with Jung. Morris L. West

(1983), in *The World is Made of Glass*, indicated that Jung frequently interviewed patients while his female assistants (who were also sometimes students) were in the room. Although West offers a fictional account of Jung, the novel is reputed to be based on historical data. If the data noted by West is factual, it raises the question about whether a nurse or other attending female person was in some way part of the treatment with this patient. If this was the case, we need to understand Jung's reason (conscious or unconscious) for including the "nurse" and to determine the effect this had on the patient. All that is reported about a woman's involvement in this case is that the patient's wife encouraged him to consult Jung. This possibility raises additional questions: did the wife communicate with Jung; what did they discuss; did they have a professional or personal relationship? These issues all have important implications for this case and for understanding the dream. Regardless of the helpful aspects of the wife's encouragement, her involvement becomes a part of the dynamics of her husband's treatment.

The dreamer (and/or his wife) may have unconsciously felt that he needed the help of Jung's feminine side, to "nurse" him back to authentic life. It may also have been that because the patient was unconscious of the inner wisdom of his own undeveloped feminine aspects, his wife suggested the association with Jung. In close relationships such as husband and wife, the process of *projective identification* (a bridging of unconscious boundaries between the two) allows one person to give voice to the other's unconscious situation. Like Athene, the goddess of wisdom born parthogenetically from her father Zeus' forehead, his wife may have sensed an inner wisdom trapped within her husband.

Another meaning of the nurse's helpful role to the doctor may be interpreted as the ego's role in helping to metabolize the contents of the Self. Archetypally, the image may refer to some need to assist the physician and patient to bring their potentialities into the world.

The next dream figure is of the fortune teller/palmist. A central theme of this image involves divination. Fortune tellers function as mediums for their client's unconscious material. However, consulting a fortune teller/palmist implies a desire to gain access to the unconscious without investing the time, money, and effort an in depth analysis requires.

In considering this case, it is curious why the patient associates to the fortune teller/palmist and how the image is connected to his unconscious perceptions of Jung and the treatment. Jung's interpretation isolates the image, seeing it as static and arising from a one-dimensional system—the patient's internal dynamics. This early method of interpretation may be completely accurate, but could be enhanced by a fuller investigation of the therapeutic setting to determine if the image corresponds primarily to the patient's unconscious perceptions of the dynamics between him and Jung, and/or if it is influenced by Jung's personal psychology. It would be of tremendous value to know the patient's conscious thoughts about Jung and Jung's approach. Had the dreamer heard rumors about Jung's method or might it seem that the approach was too much like going to a fortune teller? One could speculate and wonder if the connection between the fortune teller/palmist and the analytic relationship were a reading (albeit perhaps only partially correct) of the objective psyche's perception of Jung and his approach to treatment.

Had Jung lived long enough to join the psychoanalytic dialogue that continued after his death in 1961, he may have begun to consider additional theoretical approaches. Given his devotion to the discoveries of the psyche, Jung would likely have begun to ask additional questions regarding the workings of the psychoidal dimensions of the psyche within the therapeutic relationship. In order to integrate contemporary psychoanalytic theory, he would have needed to examine his analytic work from a different perspective. From a contemporary viewpoint, in addition to exploring the intrapsychic dynamics of his patient, he would also have had to consider the influence of the interpersonal dynamics. For example, he would have needed to investigate how the patient's experience of treatment and the effects of his own emotional states were reflected in the images emerging from the patient's psyche. Had he had the advantage of this perspective, he might subsequently have had to consider if he had been functioning inappropriately with his patient.

This reasoning brings us directly to the image of the bitter drink, the fermented milk that had to be swallowed. In presenting this image, the psyche has indicted that someone must learn a difficult truth about him or herself. In this case, Jung clearly believes that it is the patient who has to swallow this bitter truth about his disturbances. However, if the dream images reflected the patient's unconscious perception of Jung, then he (Jung), too, would have had to face a painful truth about himself, his mental health, and his unconscious motivations for conducting treatment in the manner he did. To neglect this aspect of the dream would be to create an enormous bastion against encountering the healing and perceptive qualities of the objective psyche and could result in a grave injustice to the patient.

The dream's lysis presents Jung as having no time to see the patient. Jung never commented on this in his interpretation. This image could be the patient's accurate, unconscious appraisal of the treatment situation. Because of Jung's method for conducting analysis and especially as a result of his inner turmoil during this phase of his life, he may not have been psychically available to treat this patient. It may well be that part of the bitter drink the patient must swallow was the realization and acceptance of his unconscious experience with Jung. For many patients, having to face the disturbances and pathology in their families and again in their therapists is a painful process. To avoid these perceptions, they will often assume/introject the pathology of the significant others in their lives as a method for maintaining their illusions of security and trust.

The brief clinical data we have about this patient alludes to the possibility that he suffered from an inability to acknowledge his perceptions and, in turn, lived as the designated symptomatic patient in the family. I am referring to the fact that his wife referred him to treatment and the fact that she was married to a man with mental disturbances severe enough to have required hospitalization. In many cases of the spouses of alcoholics, drug addicts, and the mentally ill, there appears to be a great secondary gain for remaining in the relationship. An unconscious reason for staying in and choosing such relationships often involves the spouse's need to identify the partner as the patient, and thus a defense against seeing his or her own madness and turmoil. Often, the therapeutic task in these cases is to highlight the entangled symbiosis between the couple and to interpret how each partner has been using the relationship for his or her own defensive needs.

Jung's interpretation of this dream might today be seen as a defense against seeing the possible truth of the patient's unconscious perception. As difficult as it may be for analysts to hear such truthful and, at times, disparaging comments about oneself, especially at a time when one is suffering his or her own conflicts, it is important to examine the interactional components of unconscious communications in the initial interview to maintain as much objectivity as possible.

A third case demonstrating Jung's approach to the initial interview is found in Jung's autobiography, *Memories, Dreams, Reflections* (1961). It involves the treatment (and subsequent termination after the third session) of a young male patient. Jung provides a brief description of the patient: "He was a doctor, and came to me with the best recommendations from an old colleague. He had been his assistant and had later taken over his practice" (p.134).

Jung's notes on the initial consultation stressed the patient's presentation of himself as normal and well adjusted, and that he sought out treatment only because of an interest in psychoanalysis.

In the second interview, the patient presented the following dream:

He dreamt that he was traveling by railroad. The train had a two-hour stop in a certain city. Since he did not know the city and wanted to see something of it, he set out toward the city center. There he found a medieval building, probably the town hall, and went into it. He wandered down long corridors and came upon handsome rooms, their walls lined with paintings and fine tapestries. Precious old objects stood about. Suddenly he saw that it had grown darker, and the sun had set. He thought, I must get back to the railroad station. At this moment he discovered that he was lost, and no longer knew where the exit was. He started in alarm, and simultaneously realized that he had not met a single person in this building. He began to feel uneasy, and quickened his pace, hoping to run into someone. But he met no one. Then he came to a large door, and thought with relief: that is the exit. He opened the door and discovered that he had stumbled upon a gigantic room. It was so huge and dark that he could not even see the opposite wall. Profoundly alarmed, the dreamer ran across the great empty room, hoping to find the exit on the other side. Then he saw-precisely in the middle of the room- something white on the floor. As he approached he discovered that it was an idiot child of about two years old. It was sitting on a chamber pot and had smeared itself with feces. (p. 135)

Writing about this dream, Jung focused on the image of the child smearing itself with feces. He writes:

I knew (from this image) all that I needed to know—here was a latent psychosis! I must say that I sweated as I tried to lead him out of the dream. I had to represent it to him as something quite innocuous, and gloss over the perilous details. (p. 135)

As a result of this second interview and the above dream, Jung felt that he had to find a way to terminate the analysis. He thought that his patient would be unable to withstand an encounter with his psychotic potential. The following dream occurred after the second interview, and was discussed in the third and final session: *"[I] was being pursued by a dangerous maniac"*(p. 136).

In this third session, Jung successfully persuaded the patient to give up the analysis, saying that he found nothing wrong with him.

This case appears much more complicated than one might imagine. Jung's fear of the patient's latent psychosis must have been a result of a number of contributing factors in his decision to terminate treatment. The dreams suggest that a psychotic core did exist in the patient. Jung reasoned that the degree of dissonance between the patient's conscious perceptions of himself and the dream's representation of him as a psychotic child and madman offered conclusive evidence for the diagnosis. Whether an in-depth analysis would have resulted in a psychotic break remains an unanswered question, although for Jung, the verdict was already in.

An important question to ask of this case material is: "What were the unconscious factors causing Jung to terminate this treatment?" Previously, I mentioned that the only material Jung provides about this patient involves his taking over the medical practice of his mentor. Jung's inclusion of this data may offer an important clue for determining his unconscious motives for refusing to treat this patient.

Jung's conflictual relationship with authority figures is an often-referenced fact, evidenced in his struggles with his father and later with Freud. In *The Freud-Jung Relationship: The Other Side of Oedipus and Countertransference* (1982), Alexander describes Jung's Oedipal struggle:

> ...he [Jung] thought that his mother really preferred him to his father. Jung did not see his father as particularly admirable: he was rather frightening in his dogmatic approach to things and thus not a figure to emulate. It is not unlikely that Jung was disappointed with him and harbored, in part, a wish for an adult male figure who could provide him with answers to his perplexing questions, but his early experiences made him wary of such a possibility. (p. 1010)

Alexander later discusses Jung's fear of a relationship with a father figure, and the possibility that his experience with his father taught him that "son-ship" required complete submission, which had to be avoided at all costs.

Jung apparently continued his unconscious search for a father and heroic ideal in his relationship with Freud. Freud became the mentor he could admire and with whom he unconsciously felt he could undergo a positive initiatory experience.

His first meeting with Freud is recorded as a thirteen-hour conversation that occurred in Vienna in 1907. Prior to this meeting, they had exchanged numerous letters and scientific papers. Their kinship endured without blemish until 1909. The event that triggered Jung's thoughts of leaving his mentor involved Freud's telling one of his dreams to Jung. When Jung asked for additional associations, Freud refused. Jung (1961) recalls this incident:

> *Freud had a dream.... I interpreted it as best I could, but added that a great deal more could be said about it if he would supply me with some additional details from his private life. Freud's response to these words was a curious look—a look of the utmost suspicion. Then he said, "But I cannot risk my authority!" At that moment, he lost it altogether. That sentence burned itself into my memory, and in it the end of our relationship was already foreshadowed. Freud was placing personal authority above truth. (p. 158)*

Freud may have unconsciously sensed his pupil's growing estrangement and made a last emotional effort to rescue Jung's respect and loyalty.

Jung felt that the time for asserting his independence from Freud was painfully close. During this period, 1910-1911, he was working on *Symbols of Transformation*, a book that he knew would eventually cause their separation. While working on this project, Jung experienced the first of what were to become a series of severe psychological (and perhaps psychotic) disturbances, all of which were activated by his need to leave Freud. He describes this disturbance:

> *For two months I was unable to touch my pen, so tormented was I by the conflict. Should I keep my thoughts to myself or should I risk the loss of so important a friendship? At last I resolved to go ahead with the writing and it did indeed cost me Freud's friendship. (p.167)*

Their relationship may also have been based on Jung's negative experiences with his own father. There were both personal and archetypally-derived reasons why Jung needed to leave Freud. This period is described in his autobiography. Freud had been grooming Jung to be his successor. This role appears to have reactivated Jung's fear of being limited and restrained, in that he knew that to follow Freud meant to sacrifice his individual pursuits. In retrospect we can now appreciate the strength of Jung's complex around the issues of freedom and constraint in relation to any father orthodoxy, especially in light of the tremendous scope of Jung's vision. He needed total freedom to bring his gifts to fruition. Jung appears to have panicked, imagining that there was no way to carve an entity of his own while still under Freud's tutelage. In part, this was a realistic perception of the Jung/Freud relationship but it was also embedded in Jung's negative father complex. Jung declined the position of Freud's theoretical and political inheritance and decided to refuse the generous offer to be his successor. Barbara Hannah (1976) describes the events that marked Jung's departure from Freud:

> *The year 1912 saw the end of the friendship; although the two men met once more (at the Munich congress in November 1913), it was no longer possible for them to reach any mutual understanding. Freud was now afraid that Jung (through his editorship of the Jahrbuch and his presidency of the International Association, into both of which he had pushed Jung against his natural bent) would keep the power in his hands and put Freud and his inner group in a difficult position. Jung had no wish whatever for that sort of power, and to Freud's great surprise and*

*relief, resigned the editorship of the Jahrbuch in October
1913, and the presidency of the International Association
in April 1914. (p.103)*

The events described above allowed Jung to break from the
Freudian inheritance and obligation. In part, Jung's decision
to follow his own clinical empiricism indicated that Freud had
lost sight of the deeper meaning of psychic material because of
his obsession with the sexual libido theory. Jung recognized
this as Freud's shortcoming and dedicated his work to following
his own clinical and theoretical explorations into the nature of
the psyche.

Jung never fully realized the symbolic act of patricide that
leaving Freud entailed. Jung symbolically had to kill Freud the
father in order to survive as a creative individual. Freud's fainting
incidents, which occurred while meeting with Jung, attest to
the highly charged unconscious field between them. I suspect
that Freud had (correctly) unconsciously perceived Jung's death
wish against him but was unable to fully consciously experience
these feelings, and that his fainting was an hysterical reaction
to this conflict.

The severity of Jung's struggle is described in his
autobiography (1961). In the chapter *"Confronting the
Unconscious,"* Jung described that he experienced what could
be diagnosed as a psychotic break. Jung apparently could not
accept his conflicting feelings for Freud any more than he could
accept the view of his father as an incompetent. As a result,
Jung unconsciously wanted to succeed Freud as patriarch of
the analytic movement. His role as editor of the *Jahrbuch* and
president of the International Association may point to his
desire to overtake Freud's place. Initially, these positions allowed
Jung to champion Freud's causes, but in time, the wish to
succeed him surfaced. We can begin to understand that the
dynamics underlying the tangled relationship Jung had with
Freud were temporally (subjectively) motivated by the
relationship he had with his own father. However, underscoring
both was Jung's ongoing relationship with the "Father"
archetype that needed to be integrated into his life.

In Jung's presentation of the interviews with the young doctor, we are struck by the fact that all he chose to discuss about the patient was the issue of succession of the father. This could reveal Jung's entrainment with the patient, in that Jung too struggled with the unconscious complex of taking overtaking the authority from his father/mentor. One wonders if Jung was displacing his need to kill the father by killing (ending) the relationship with the patient. The intervention below captures what may have been Jung's unconscious undermining of the patient.

The patient's initial dream of finding a baby sitting in a room playing with its feces was presented after the initial interview. Jung may have already communicated his internal distress to the patient in the first session and, in part, the dream could be taken as a perception of this part of Jung's psyche. In that first session, Jung made a rather strange comment to the patient. The following intervention had been made in response to the patient's expressed interest in becoming an analyst. Jung said:

> *Do you know what that means? It means that you must first learn to know yourself. You yourself are the instrument. If you are not right, how can the patient be made right? If you are not convinced, how can you convince him? You yourself must be the real stuff. If you are not, God help you! Then you will lead patients astray. Therefore, you must first accept an analysis of yourself. (p. 134)*

The degree of affect implied in this intervention points to a strong emotional reaction (a complex) generated in Jung by this case. One must wonder why Jung talks about leading patients astray, and that the therapist must be "right" before trying to help patients. I believe that Jung's comments were his own unconscious perceptions the he was leading this patient astray and that he was not emotionally "right" during this work. The dream image of the baby playing with feces could be understood as the patient's unconscious perceptions of Jung's intrapsychic turmoil during the treatment, expressed consciously and unconsciously through his interventions and internal attitude about the patient. The baby could also represent a very young and troubled aspect of Jung's psyche that had never fully healed after his separation from Freud, nor from his mother's significant psychological illness and hospitalization when Jung was three years old.

The dream of being pursued by a madman occurred importantly after the second analytic session. The dream suggests that the patient unconsciously saw Jung behaving like a madman in wanting him to leave treatment and giving the questionable intervention in the first session. On a subjective level, the dream reflects the patient's disturbance, which may have begun surfacing during treatment. However, given the sequential or co-occurring processes of the patient/therapist dynamics, it is impossible to determine if the dream image is a presentation of the patient's disturbances or a reflection of his unconscious perceptions of Jung.[3] Jung interpreted the dreams solely from the subjective standpoint as would have been expected by the theoretical psychoanalytic understanding at that time. From a more contemporary perspective informed by the bi-personal dynamics of psychotherapy, his interpretation of the case could also represent an unconscious attempt to insulate himself from re-experiencing his own internal terror.

In one respect, Jung exercised sound judgment in terminating this case, because he may have unconsciously recognized that he was emotionally unable to conduct a meaningful analysis at that time. Whether or not he was aware that he was influenced by an unsolved powerful father complex is unknown.

The review of this case is valuable because it explores the initial interview situation as unconsciously attuned with Jung's historical background. The result suggests an interactive validation of the patient's unconscious observation of Jung's psychological functioning. The patient's dreams revealed disturbance, danger, and terror because he unconsciously perceived the workings of powerful unmetabolized contents within Jung's psyche. The dreams however, alerted the patient to this fact and created a situation where the analysis had to be terminated. These dreams were not simply the product of the patient's internal disturbances, but also were an accurate portrayal of his unconscious experience of Jung.

It is in keeping with Jung's respect for psyche to ask the deeper meaning of a dream or any other unconscious material presented in the initial interview. To begin and end one's interpretive activity by examining patient's material from the subjective perspective represents, in my opinion, only a partial understanding. One needs to ask the teleological question, and wonder why a particular dream, image, or derivative appears in the first session. Unconscious material does not exist in a vacuum. It arises in response to an alive and vital experience of internal and external reality. In *Two Essays on Analytical Psychology* (1953), Jung demonstrates his sensitivity for listening to unconscious material as it relates to the analytical relationship. This involves a dream he had in response to his work with a female patient, whom he had been viewing as immoral and crude. In the dream he had to look up at her. He felt the dream appeared as a compensation for his faulty conscious perceptions of the patient. This example demonstrates that when Jung was not threatened, he was able to see psychic functioning working on an interactional as well as an intrapsychic level.

There are many reasons why analysts fail to listen to unconscious material in the initial interview. Jung's case illustrates that he may have unconsciously refused to listen to the patient's unconscious perceptions because to do so would have meant that he would have to face his unresolved unconscious terrors. Guggenbühl-Craig presents one of the many factors contributing to the breakdown of a secure analytic setting. Some of these disturbances stem from personal issues such as complexes, while others stem from archetypal sources like the sorcerer projection onto the analyst. In *Power and the Helping Professions* (1978), Guggenbühl-Craig discusses this point:

> The patient's expectations and hopes of finding a powerful sorcerer also plays some part in the choice of analyst. The

analyst, of course, finds it extremely difficult not to be affected by this magician projection. In fact, he even stimulates it in the patient by trying to stress his own power and prestige. When the patient tells him of his troubles, the analyst lets it be seen that he already understands everything. Through the use of certain gestures, such as a sage nodding of the head, and of pregnant remarks introjected among the patient's statements, the analyst creates the impression that, while he may not be prepared to communicate all his knowing and profound thoughts, he has already plumbed the very depths of his patient's soul. (p. 39)

Disturbances in the frame are unavoidable and at times can even stimulate analytic progress. However, listening to patient's unconscious communications in the initial interview will help therapists recognize the presence of unmetabolized archetypal constellations within both patient and therapist that will affect the trajectory of the treatment. What we must remember is that patients demonstrate extreme sensitivity to the analytic setting. Research indicates this as an unequivocal fact and for this reason, a concern for patient's unconscious perceptions and experiences is a necessary and vital part of the analytic relationship.

Chapter 6

Case of a Child Analysis and the Patient's Response to Disruptions to the Therapeutic Relationship

This clinical vignette is taken from the treatment of a ten-year-old boy named Phil. He has a brother two years younger. Phil's mother brought him for treatment due to concern about his anti-social behavior in school. She believed that his acting out was a response to her recent divorce from Phil's father. The referral source for this case was one of my graduate students. I asked to see the boy alone for the initial interview, to which the mother agreed.

Clinical Vignette: First Session

After I introduced myself, Phil began pacing around the office, asking, *"Where is it? Where is it?"* He looked under the desk and the chairs, still asking, *"Where is it?"*

Interspersed with his asking, *"Where is it?"* were references to his mother, such as, *"Where is she?"* and *"Will she pick me up after the session?"* As his movements grew to a frenzied pace, he suddenly asked, *"Where is the tape recorder?"*

Initially, his suspicions confused me because I was not using a tape recorder and did not plan to present this material to anyone except my supervisor. (It is interesting to note that after Phil's termination, I chose to write up the case. Perhaps, on some level, he may have intuited what I would do with his material.)

I asked if his search for the tape recorder and his concern that I was hiding something had to do with his thoughts about my discussion with his mother in the initial phone call. Suddenly, he looked relieved and asked, *"What did she tell you?"* I explained all of the details of that conversation, saying that his mother had discussed his lying, fighting, starting fires in school, and bedwetting. I reluctantly divulged the latter material. I was concerned that he would feel ashamed by this, but decided to mention it, believing that it would be best for him to know everything his mother had discussed with me. I explained that, in the future, I would tell him at the beginning of each session if I had discussed anything about him with anyone else. He replied that he was not wetting the bed any more.

After this discussion, he began playing a game he had brought with him. It involved decoding a number of different symbols and putting them into words. He said, *"I'm pretty good at decoding things; I usually figure out what these difficult things mean,"* and he smiled. After playing with the game a little longer, he began talking about the room, saying how much he liked the office and wondering if he could move in.

I believe that his description of the decoding game, which occurred after our discussion about his mother's involvement in the treatment, could be taken as a positive validation of the interpretation. The decoding game, which involved understanding the meaning of symbolic images, was a reference to my attempts at comprehending his unconscious, derivative perceptions about the treatment. His relaxed behavior and thoughts of moving into my office (his manifest, conscious communications), could also be seen as his unconscious recognition that, in rectifying the situation regarding his mother's involvement in the therapy, the treatment had become safe and protective. For him to begin experiencing treatment as secure was an important step, especially in light of his reactions to the discord in the parental home.

This first session marked Phil's unconscious attempts to reveal the implications of my not having told him about the telephone conversation I had with his mother. What initially appeared as his resistance to treatment was in fact his objectively valid unconscious response to the therapeutic setting, which was experienced as dangerous and threatening. As long as I withheld his mother's information from him, therapy would remain a contaminated environment.

After the session, Phil went into the waiting room while I brought his mother into my office to discuss fees, times, and other ground rules.

Second Session

Phil was clearly depressed as he entered the office. He talked about all the fights he had seen between his parents. He recalled one particularly violent fight, which occurred in the room adjacent to his. He kept his ear to the door throughout the fight. He said, *"I felt helpless and wanted to scream."* Then he suddenly asked what I had discussed with his mother during the last session when I brought her into the office. He then talked about liars and cheaters, how angry he was with his mother for bringing different men into the house, and how this made him feel terrible.

I commented on his feeling helpless and scared when his parents fought in an adjacent room, on his anger over his mother bringing different men into his house, and on his reference to liars and cheaters. I said that last session I had brought his mother into the therapy room, which was adjacent to the room he was in. I wondered if he had felt like I was fighting with his mother, and whether that left him feeling helpless and scared. I also asked if he felt that my bringing his mother into the room was painful, and perhaps wrong, and that like his mother's tendency to bring other men into their home, I had taken his private space in treatment and made it more public. I then asked if he felt that I was a liar and cheat because in the last session I had said that if I had any communications with his mother or anyone else I would tell him what we talked about. Perhaps my failure to do so in the beginning of this session had made me appear untrustworthy. He started making karate movements showing how strong he was. He revealed that while I was talking with his mother last session, he had pressed his ear to the door and wanted to scream because of how much he hated hearing us talk together. Then he noticed a box of finger paints on the shelf and asked if he could draw. He took out the paints and began playing. He looked relaxed and content. *"My mother's not here now"*, he said, and grinned.

He painted a green ghost, and then mixed all the colors together. He tacked the picture to the wall, saying that he had dressed as a ghost for Halloween and that was pretty scary. Next he commented that it was wrong to mix all these colors together. *"I shouldn't let these different colors run into each other like this."*

I talked about the picture: *"It sounds as though something scared you, and I wonder if it has to do with my bringing your mother into the room last session with you being here, too. When you said that it was wrong to let all the colors run together, I wonder if you may be feeling that I shouldn't let things run together, like letting your mother and you both use this therapy room. I didn't keep things separate, and I wonder if you wished that this could be your room and not your mother's."* He responded with an affirmative yes, and resumed finger painting.

Commentary on the Second Session

This session opened with a clear and close derivative representation of Phil's unconscious perceptions of my allowing his mother into the treatment room without him being present. The emergence of this material points to his unconscious sensitivity toward the securing and breaking of the treatment space. Having allowed his mother to be present without him was a mistake, in that it invalidated what I tried to convey in the first session regarding the privacy and confidentiality of our relationship.

The incident with his mother and me triggered the recall of his trauma over his parents' fight. These arguments left him terribly afraid that his security (home, parents) would be lost. In part, he imagined that his parents would eventually kill one another. These parental battles also made him afraid of his own feelings, because he feared that a show of emotion could escalate into violence.

Ghost and Mixing of Colors

It was interesting that Phil began finger painting after my intervention. The interpretation appeared to relieve his sense of being unprotected in the treatment, thus allowing him to resume symbolic communication.

In *Structure and Dynamics of the Psyche* (1916), Jung comments on the meaning of the symbol of ghost: "The unconscious imago, which no longer has an object to correspond to it, becomes a ghost and now exerts influences on the subject which cannot be distinguished in principle from psychic phenomena" (pp. 274-75).

Jung's description connects the ghost's appearance to the loss of an external object. The object is able to contain the psychic contents, whereas with the loss of the object, the container, which housed the content, is now destroyed, causing the unconscious material to exist as a homeless, ghostlike entity. The appearance of the ghost drawing is related to the patient's unconscious experiences of the breakdown in both his home and within the therapy. In many respects he not only lost his home and the sense of an intact family, but now also his therapist. We were all now without form or substance, and all had a certain ghost-like quality to us.

As a result of my not discussing with Phil the content of his mother's initial conversation, he experienced the analytic container as excessively porous. As the therapeutic *temenos* disintegrates, so too, does the patient's internal world. My initial attempts at rectifying the situation temporarily restored

Phil's trust in the analysis. However, by allowing Phil's mother to enter the treatment room (without him), I undid the corrective measures of the previous intervention. The positive holding capacities of the treatment had dissolved, resulting in the patient's depression. He was now psychically vulnerable, perceiving the therapist as unpredictable and unable to provide the security needed to carry out a meaningful analysis. Unconsciously, Phil hoped that the therapist could provide the stability that had been so desperately lacking in the home. Phil could only begin exploring his frightening feelings about his family as well as the images from his internal world when the therapist provided a structure that he could see as being less frightening and more benevolent than his parental environment.

Phil's comment about the colors running into one another represents his unconscious perception that the boundaries within the analysis had become blurred. This dissolution caused Phil unconsciously to view the analyst as functioning in an undifferentiated and destructive way. The analyst failed to clearly separate his relationship to the patient from his relationship to the patient's mother. At this stage of Phil's development, he needed to become more differentiated in his responses to his parents concerning his feelings about the divorce. In order to achieve a differentiated conscious response, he will have to introject the healthy conscious functioning of a significant other. Neither the mother nor father could offer the child such an introjective experience, because they both functioned on such an unconscious level and continually failed to provide security or meaning in their child's life. Especially in child analysis, the analytic space and the analyst's ability to maintain it become the (corrective parental) *imagos* for the patient. If the analyst can successfully maintain the therapeutic setting, the child will learn through identification how to protect himself and to develop a differentiated and conscious reaction to the family chaos. In the face of a breakdown in analytic security, the patient often withdraws, disappointed that yet another person is unable to protect him. To allow the mother to contaminate the child's treatment space represented an undifferentiated intervention, which, to a large extent, was responsible for the emergence of the ghost imagery.

The Holy Ghost of Christian symbolism is believed to symbolize the divine spark, or sudden inspiration. It represents the eruption into consciousness of an unconscious content.[1] Gnostic theology describes the Holy Ghost as a symbol of the missing feminine element in the Blessed Trinity. Phil colored the ghost emerald green. Jung, in *Psychology and Religion* (1937), draws a connection between the Holy Ghost and the color green. He writes: "The golden color...belongs to the father, the red to the son, and the green to the holy ghost (p. 69).

In *Mysterium Coniunctionis* (1963), Jung comments that: "green is the color of the holy ghost, of life of procreation and resurrection...it signifies hope" (p. 289).

Jung's interpretation of the Holy Ghost and the color green points to the potential health of the patient. However, this growth will be hindered as long as the analytic structure continues to violate Phil's need for privacy and protection.

It is important to note that Phil tacked the picture to the office wall, suggesting the possibility of his need to be seen and to have a mirror transference experience in therapy. However, we also have to consider the possibility that hanging the picture may also be expressive of his unconscious awareness that the therapy had become more public, and thus less safe.

Following this session, there were two missed appointments. The first absence was due to Phil's coming down with the flu. His mother took him and his brother on vacation during the second week. It is interesting that after the appearance of the ghost, Phil became ill. This raises the possibility that the unmetabolized psychic content symbolized by the ghost had infected his system. His inability to fight off the virus indicates a breakdown in his immune response. He may have unconsciously introjected the breakdown of the analytic relationship. I was surprised that Phil's mother scheduled a vacation so soon after his beginning treatment. This suggests an unconscious opposition to her son's recovery.

Five minutes before the next scheduled appointment, his mother called to say that she would not be able to get Phil to the session because the person who was to drive her had not yet arrived. She asked if I could schedule a later appointment. I recommended that we maintain the original times unless she felt it was absolutely necessary to reschedule. While we were still on the phone, her friend arrived and they left for my office. They arrived fifteen minutes late.

When he arrived, Phil again looked sad. He said, *"It's been a long time since I've seen you."* We talked about this for a bit, and I told him about his mother's phone call and my suggestion that we stick to the original time. His material at this session remained flat, as did his affect. At the end of the appointment he handed me a check for the month. However, the payment did not include the missed appointments, a policy his mother and I had agreed to in the initial interview. After the session, I called her to discuss it. She said she thought she had to pay, but was not sure, and would include the additional money in next month's check.

The next day, Phil's mother left a message on my answering machine, explaining that she was terminating treatment because she refused to pay for missed appointments and the scheduled appointment time was too difficult to keep. I was in a difficult therapeutic position. The mother's decision revealed her unconscious wish to destroy her son's treatment. If her son's best interests were her primary concern, she could have handled these concerns differently. I felt that she wanted to control me and the analysis, implying that treatment would be under her terms or not at all. She probably felt that I was doing the same thing, which threw us into a nasty power play. From the material I gathered about her marriage, it appeared that she constantly belittled her husband, which stimulated many of their fights. The husband provoked the fights by behaving irresponsibly. My dilemma was: if I altered the ground rules to accommodate the mother's request (and hopefully to continue Phil's treatment), Phil would have a legitimate reason to equate me with his father, in that we were both unable to handle the mother's authority. My concern was that Phil would be unable to see me as competent because I behaved like his father. If I held fast to the ground rules (because I believed they would help Phil), the mother would surely terminate treatment. In either case, Phil was the victim. When I called Phil's mother, she said she was sorry to end the treatment because Phil had shown such great improvement during the brief time he saw me. I asked if she would reconsider her decision if I waived the policy for missed sessions and arranged for a later time. She quickly agreed to these terms and we set up another time.

There were a number of contributing factors in wanting to continue working with Phil. I liked him and felt that I had an understanding of his problems; I also wanted further experience working with children. In addition, even though this was a very low fee treatment, we had to consider the therapist's financial benefits in accepting this case as another contributing factor.

Prior to the next appointment, Phil's mother called to say that he was acting up in school again: fighting, lighting fires, and lying. She asked if I would call his teacher. She could not understand why he was having problems because he had been doing so well since beginning treatment.

I was annoyed by her naiveté and her behavior, which to a large extent contributed to the undermining of this treatment. I believed that on some level she had to understand the relationship between her sabotage of Phil's treatment (the termination request) and the resurgence of his symptoms. I had to also realize that the breakdown in analytic security also played a central role in the resurgence of his symptoms. There were many different levels to my response to Phil's mother. Clearly, she evoked a strong emotional reaction in me that had to be understood. (Admittedly, I do admire Phil's mother for shouldering the financial responsibility of the treatment. Phil's father declined to provide support. Also, she was concerned enough to find help for her son.)

I explained to her that it would be best if I confined my relationship to just Phil and myself, and that talking to his teacher would serve as a distraction to our work. In retrospect, I was naïve in not realizing that to protect the treatment, I had to establish an alliance with the mother as well as the son. I also realize now that an ideal frame is just that—an ideal to aim for. It cannot be fully achieved with children. Disruptions are the norm and need to be tolerated by the therapist. By not understanding this earlier, I became further alienated from the mother.

As Phil sat down to begin the session, I explained that I had recently talked with his mother and that we had agreed on a new financial arrangement about missed sessions. I told him that this would be our time, and that I would not be talking with his teacher, as his mother had requested. With the simplistic wisdom found in children, he said, *"There sure have been a lot of phone calls."* The rest of the material in the session was flat, containing little if any meaning.

During the week, the mother again called, urging me to talk with the teacher. This time, partly out of frustration, I agreed. I talked with his teacher, explaining that I was aware of his problems in school and that we were working on them.

When Phil arrived for the following session, I told him about the calls from his mother and my calls to his teacher. A sadness came over him as I said this. He responded that he did not believe in Santa Claus anymore. He then looked around the room to see if his picture was on the wall. He asked, *"Have people seen my picture?"* Then he started talking about his father, saying that he could not understand his actions. He described his father's new house, and said he was allowed to help cut some of the boards for the floor. He added that, out of the blue, his father had decided to sell the house. Phil kept saying, *"Why is he selling it? Why is he giving our house away?"* He talked about how special the house had been and how he was going to miss it. Then he talked about a horror movie he had seen where men were vaporized.

I intervened, asking if he also was speaking of his feelings about the new financial arrangements, my agreement to change the therapy time, and my decision to call his teacher. I asked if he felt I was talking about him to others and exposing our work together (derivatively expressed with the reference of my showing his pictures to others). Perhaps he felt he could not trust or believe in me anymore, like he could not believe in Santa Claus? I wondered if all the changes in our relationship made him feel that I was taking something away that had been important to him, like his father's sudden decision to sell the house. I added that, because of all these changes, perhaps he was feeling that something we had been building together—our relationship (like his father's house)—was being taken away. Perhaps because of this, he felt that I had died or vaporized, much as his father had disappeared from his everyday life.

After this session, I realized that there was yet another dimension to the image of vaporized men. Following the second interview, I had decided to take supervision on this case. My supervisor strongly recommended that unless the patient produced derivative communication, I should remain silent. While I sensed that this interventional style could perhaps be difficult for a child to manage, I decided to follow his suggestion. So the image of the vaporized men and of his father selling the house may also represent the patient's unconscious perception of the therapist selling out his own innate beliefs about the case, and in turn destroying treatment. In many respects, my behavior may well have mirrored the father's inability to stand up for his own beliefs and creations, as suggested by his selling the house that he and the son both loved. I have spent a great deal of time carefully considering why I allowed this supervisory introject to override my own clinical stance in this case. This was Phil's final session. His mother called saying he did not want to come to the sessions any longer.

The material in this final session indicates that Phil was unconsciously working over his mother's attempt to terminate treatment and his feeling that, because of all the disturbances in the therapy, meaningful work had ended. The images of the house being taken away and the vaporized men are unconscious perceptions of termination and of the therapist, respectively, in light of my participation in the demise of the treatment. My inconsistent behavior was triggered by the mother's threats to take her son out of therapy. Phil was torn by his feelings of loyalty toward his mother and resentment toward his father. Phil's sense of loss was overwhelming. As the treatment situation began repeating the dynamics in his own family, he withdrew. In part, this was due to Phil's terror of seeing a collapse in security and to his unconscious recognition that I, like his father, failed to neutralize his mother's aggression. In his eyes, I was another weak male, unable to build and maintain a home for him in which to feel secure.

If I had the chance to re-do this case, I would handle it quite differently. To begin with, I would have suggested that the mother find a therapist to work with. This could have offset the toxic effect she had on her son's treatment. She was a disturbed woman, shackled with tremendous responsibilities. She doubted her ability to handle the pressures of being a single parent. I should have agreed to talk with Phil's teacher, and I should have changed the appointment time when the mother explained the problem. I am still not sure how I would handle the policy about payment for missed sessions. My experience has been that payment represents an arrangement that patients and therapists unconsciously feel adds stability to the treatment.

The frightening images from Phil's internal world receded as the structure and security of the analysis fell apart. The *temenos* he so desperately needed had been destroyed. His terror receded deep within his psyche. The lack of significant material in the final sessions attests to the resistance that set in to protect Phil from exposing his wounds in such a damaged setting.

I believe that a different sort of frame from what I offered this patient was necessary to handle the complexities of the case. This frame would have to be responsive to the mother's psychological state and her request for "special conditions of treatment", yet firm enough to create an analytic attitude to examine the affects of these conditions on Phil. I feel that my inability to satisfy both these analytic tasks contributed to his premature termination.

At the very beginning of treatment, Phil exhibited substantial progress and there was a temporary resolution of his symptoms. I understand the relationship between the mother's disruption of the therapy and the reemergence of Phil's symptoms, but because of the complications within the analytic setting an in-depth working through of the issues did not occur.

Perhaps if I had maintained a secure frame, even in light of the mother's threats of termination, I would have helped to strengthen a positive introject of the maternal environment.

In reviewing this material, I am struck by the power of the patient's unconscious to clearly spell out the implications of changes within the treatment, and by his unconscious attempts to rectify the situation, in hopes of creating a safe rehabilitative environment.

CHAPTER 7

INITIAL INTERVIEW: A STUDY OF A PATIENT'S IMMUNE DEFICIENCY AND ITS RELATIONSHIP TO HER CHOICE OF A TREATMENT SETTING

The immune system is the biological correlate of humankind's psychological efforts at self-preservation.[1] From the immune system's autonomous response to the presence of toxic elements, we have learned that certain substances and relationships enhance development, whereas others represent a serious threat.

When an antigen is detected within the body, the immune system signals a survival response, which is manifested by the activation of an immunological reaction. Antibodies are created to destroy the specific antigen they combat. What is especially interesting in the study of immuno-reactions is the specificity utilized in the creation of antibodies. They are created to match the molecular composition of the target antigen. This demonstrates that physiologically an individual (organism) possesses the capacity to recognize and to appropriate the significance of a pathological situation; the organism's response is specifically tailored to the kind of crisis that must be managed in order to survive. This capability is instinctively inherent in all of us.

The autonomy of the immune system's functioning parallels the ego-Self relationship, which creates a type of psychoimmunological response system. The Self acts to protect the ego by alerting it to the presence of non-Self/toxic elements in the psyche. The Self communicates these perceptions to the ego by way of physical and verbal analogies—compensatory dreams, psychosomatic disorders, surges of affect, or derivative communications.

The case discussed in this chapter presents an initial consultation and follow-up session with a twenty-six year old female patient (Dee), seeking treatment at a low-cost therapy clinic. The patient worked for a satellite organization of the clinic, which was housed in the same building as the therapy center. She knew a number of staff people in common with the therapist.

As the therapist greeted the patient for the initial interview, he found her sitting and talking with the clinic secretary. Dee began the session by talking about her relationship with this secretary, saying that they had known each other for some time. Then she discussed her reasons for beginning treatment:

> "I've had a problem with my immune system since I was a child. I've been seeing a doctor but haven't gotten any better. I'm often sick, since I'm unable to ward off disease.
>
> One of the reasons for starting therapy has to do with unresolved feelings about my father. He was always cruel and destructive to me. Often when I would tell him things in confidence, he would turn around and tell my friends what we discussed. I hated him for it. Much of the time, I thought he was insane. One time he came after me with a chain saw. I really thought he'd kill me if he ever caught up with me. You had to be afraid of him, 'cause he was almost always out of control. I had to keep my distance from him.
>
> I've been concerned about this trainee working at the clinic, who's been coming on to me. I really don't want to get involved with him. I'm feeling uncomfortable talking about this relationship because you know him."

The therapist commented on the horror she must have felt in her relationship with her father, and acknowledged her need for wanting treatment. He added, however, that she indicated a reservation about undergoing therapy at this site, evidenced by her not wanting to talk about her relationship with the trainee.

The therapist went on to comment on her description of a violent relationship with a man who threatened her life, and who constantly betrayed her confidence by revealing her secrets to her friends. He asked if these feelings and experiences could also be related to her coming to the clinic for treatment, where they both know people in common. Perhaps she felt that he was going to betray her trust, and that there were things she could not discuss because of their mutual acquaintances. He added that she may have a strong unconscious feeling that the conditions of therapy were now violent and abusive because of the lack of security. The session ended with an agreement to have a second consultation to further examine her feelings about treatment.

This patient was bright, articulate, and sincere in her desire to begin therapy. In many respects, she was a good candidate for analysis. However, the therapist's enthusiasm for working on this case was tempered by Dee's unconscious material, which revealed serious concerns about the advisability of continuing treatment.

The material about her immune disturbance offered an important insight into her unconscious experience of the treatment setting as a toxic environment against which she had no defenses. Initially, the immune system serves to warn of the presence of toxicity and to initiate a response to the antigen. Because of Dee's immune deficiency, she was unable to create a physiological response that either recognizes or wards off a physically harmful situation. The therapist speculated that the traumatic relationship with her father triggered the breakdown of Dee's immune system. To have been continually victimized by him may have caused her to feel desperate and hopeless of ever finding protection or understanding. In *Immunity: The Double Edged Sword*, Schmeck (1974) describes the breakdown of the immune system: "it is almost as though the body finally wearies of the self-non-self argument that [it] has been carrying on with its environment for a lifetime" (p. 131).

Dee's physiological condition mirrored the psychological state of victimization. She described in that first consultation the experience of herself as helpless against damaging environmental conditions. She had gone into therapy in a clinic where she would literally be unable to prevent damaging speculations by her colleagues; where she had no control over her environment, and could not trust the therapist to protect her.

Second Interview

An interesting event occurred the day before Dee's second appointment. The therapist called the director of the organization she worked for. Dee answered the phone and put the therapist on hold. However, she then picked up his extension again, thinking it was the call she had been having with her friend. She said, "The strangest thing just happened. My shrink called and is on the other line." When the therapist interjected, she said that she thought she was still talking with her friend. This was an embarrassing situation, with important implications for the therapeutic relationship. One had to wonder how this would affect the next appointment.

Dee began the session by describing her living arrangement. She shared an apartment with a number of roommates, but had come to realize that she wanted a place of her own. Also the landlord lived directly above her, and constantly spied on her comings and goings. She said, "I feel there's just no privacy; I can't live my own life under these conditions. I wish I had my own apartment." She then related the following dream:

The Dream

I am living in an apartment complex. My parents live in the next apartment. Suddenly, there is a nuclear explosion. Everything is destroyed except my apartment. I'm shocked to see so much devastation, but am grateful that I have been saved.

Her Associations

Apartment: Where I'm presently living feels like an apartment complex. We virtually live on top of one another.

Apartment Complex: I've never really liked them; all the units are the same; nothing is unique or special.

Parents: We have never been close. I've told you about my father already. He was pretty violent to me. I can't understand why we're living next door to one another. My mother was interested in me, but I never fully respected her.

Nuclear explosion: The worst of all possible disasters. Makes me think of the complete devastation in the movie *The Day After*. Being saved from the explosion— this just doesn't make any sense. If there really was a nuclear explosion, no one would be saved.

After giving the above associations, she mentioned that she was thinking about the last appointment, and wondered what was happening in therapy. They then talked about the previous day's phone incident, connecting it to her references of having no privacy and of the landlord spying on her. He wondered if his call may have made her feel that she had no privacy from the therapist—that he was spying on her. He also discussed how her feelings about the treatment seemed to be making her feel confined, and that might have been similar to the feelings she had about her inability psychologically to separate from her parents.

The dream represented Dee's internal dynamics as well as her perceptions of the therapeutic situation. It takes place in an apartment building, suggesting a lack of differentiation. This point is emphasized by the image of her parents living next door. A third reference to this lack of differentiation can be seen in the immune disturbance (as mentioned earlier). The dreamer has been unable to establish a personal psychology separate from her parental introjects and, in general, a separate, autonomous ego structure.

They talked about the nuclear explosion in the dream-that this could refer to the trauma she had experienced with her father's active death wish and violent actions against her. Another way to understand this dream image is to see it as a statement of her intense fear of having to face and relive this traumatic event. She was, perhaps, unconsciously feeling that to face the realization of her father's actions against her could seriously jeopardize her psychological stability.

As we consider the fact that everyone within the apartment complex would have been destroyed by a nuclear explosion, we can surmise that there is a tremendous denial system at work suggesting that devastating effects can be avoided. This denial is operative within her relationship to own family and her past history, the consequences and decisions in her current life, and within treatment. Specifically she and the therapist had to work over the potentially devastating effects of the lack of security and confidentiality in the treatment relationship. By being spared annihilation, she had avoided a confrontation with her internal world, just as by shunning intimate relationships in her external life, she had escaped experiencing the terror a relationship would surely evoke for her.

Winnicott (1935) believes that virtually any action that helps the patient to avoid depression and annihilation anxieties represents a manic defensive stance. In describing the manic defense he writes: "[The Manic defense is] the employment of almost any opposites in the reassurance against death, chaos, and mystery" (pp. 143-144). He also states: "The Manic defense is intended to cover a person's capacity to deny depressive anxiety that is inherent in emotional development, anxiety that belongs to the capacity of the individual to feel guilt" (pp. 143-144). "Might it be that the main point...is a denial of deadness, a defense against depressive death..." (p. 131).

The therapist tried to be extremely careful and sensitive with his interpretation of the dream and her unconscious thoughts about this treatment because they could have been taken as a rejection. He said he believed that her desire for treatment was sincere, and encouraged her to find a therapist

and to begin analysis. He discussed all the references she had
made to apartment complexes—having to share an apartment
with others and the desire to find her own place, as possibly
indicating the need to find a private therapeutic setting with
someone that was not now or previously in direct contact with
her in her professional or personal life. (She had resources to
afford private treatment.) After the interview, she did consult
an analyst in private practice.

This case has been instructive for a number of reasons. It
demonstrates a patient's unconscious perceptions of the
therapeutic setting as presented in the initial interview. These
perceptions are conveyed to both patient and analyst through
derivative communication and dreams. This material also
suggests that certain conditions of treatment are necessary to
provide patients with a secure analytic setting. This hints at
the possibility of there being an *a priori* set of conditions of
treatment. Lastly, this case illustrates the patient's use of a
contaminated treatment setting as an externalization of her
manic defenses.

Regardless of whether other therapists would have accepted
this case for ongoing treatment, I am presenting this material
to demonstrate the ability of the unconscious to clearly and
accurately describe the unconscious implications of a treatment
occurring under less than ideal conditions. The unconscious
alerted both patient and therapist to the meaning of this
therapy, and offered the patient the following insights:

1. her need to find treatment where healing would be
possible

2. her attraction to relationships that repeated the
violence she had experienced with the father

3. the relationship between her immune deficiency
and its psychological correlate.

It is possible that under certain therapeutic situations where
"special conditions of treatment" prevail, meaningful analytic
work could be accomplished. There is also a possibility that
the similarity between the patient's original trauma with the

father and her unconscious concerns about this treatment could have been analyzed and worked through. However, because of the newness of the therapist's insights about the initial interview situation, he was not prepared to take this next step of beginning treatment. (At the actual time of the case, he felt he worked to the best of his ability and knowledge of the patient's material and of unconscious communication, thus feeling that his interpretation and the therapeutic experience were of value to the patient and an important learning experience for him.)[2]

In this particular case, the breaks in the frame served to support the patient's manic defenses, thus causing the therapist to offer a guarded prognosis to treatment under these conditions. This caused a sectoring off of the memories and effects around the trauma with her father and inhibited the flow of unconscious material related to the traumatic episode. The relationship between the manic defense and the patient's denial of unconscious processes is described by Winnicott (1975): "It is part of one's manic defense to be unable to give full significance to their inner reality. There are fluctuations in one's ability to respect inner reality that are directly related to the depressive anxiety in oneself" (p. 129).

Winnicott's position on the importance of inner reality in the patient's healing process echoes Jung's belief that analysis has to include a meaningful relationship to the unconscious. To have a manic defensive structure built into the analytic container inevitably shuts patients off from their internal reality.

In this case, I have discussed the patient's need to re-experience the traumas from her relationship with her father— not to suggest that this would be the only meaningful analytic work, but to highlight the relationship between the ego's ability to tolerate facing internal terror and the development of a meaningful relationship with the Self. As trauma is repressed, so too is the possibility of any healing influence from the Self.

CHAPTER 8

MORPHOGENETIC DYNAMICS IN THE ANALYTIC RELATIONSHIP[1]

It has been repeatedly pointed out that Jung's notion of the archetype as psychic form in potential would have benefited from the last fifty years of research into the nature of material existence. I believe that the therapist/patient relationship can be profitably discussed as an archetypal configuration of elements, whose properties can be better understood by bringing Jung's ideas into dialogue with recent theories about biological form (Sheldrake 1981, 1984, 1988; Goodwin 1972, 1978, 1983, 1986) and the new physics (Laszlo 1987, 1988; Zukav 1979; Morris 1983).

The therapist/patient relationship is generally discussed in terms of the interpersonal dynamics generated within it. However, as Langs has demonstrated, the clinical elements of therapy can also be described as a system—a bi-personal field determined as much by system parameters as by the psyches of patient and therapist. That is, a therapeutic exchange is created not only by the relationship of the participants, but by the forms and structure of the environment or field in which the dyad is operating. As a system, the therapeutic process is liable to the same questions about form and development that are currently being framed in the biological and physical sciences.

Sheldrake's Theory of Formative Causation

Sheldrake's hypothesis of formative causation has recently caught the attention of the Jungian community, and his work is now being cited in numerous Jungian publications. It not only proposes a scientific basis for Jung's understanding of collective memory, but would extend the concept of the archetype beyond psychology to account for the consistency and stability of all material forms.

Sheldrake postulates what he calls a *morphogenetic field*, which not only exists beyond space and time, but also consists of patterns produced by the forms of things that occur within space and time. In essence, anything that takes shape for the first time is held to establish a resonance pattern, whose existence encourages, under similar circumstances, a self-similar amalgamation of elements. Each time the same configuration of elements occurs, the level of morphogenetic resonance increases, thus increasing both the ease and likelihood of that form's reoccurrence. The more times a form has actually occurred, the greater the pattern's resonance: the more resonance, the more stable the form will become. Certain forms that we take for granted—oak trees, chickens, roses—are virtually unchanging because their morphogenetic resonance is so high.

The morphogenetic field is assumed to exist because no one has discovered, in the basic elements that constitute the building blocks of material development, any property that could determine the specific form of the finished product. For example, DNA contains coding for protein production, but it contains no chemical instructions for the form an organism ultimately takes. Sheldrake likens DNA to the bricks needed to construct a house. Although the bricks are the material elements used to build the house, the form the house ultimately takes is not determined by the bricks. In the same way, he suggests, an acorn carries the material elements of the developing oak tree, but does not carry any kind of chemical blueprint for the oak tree's particular form. According to Sheldrake, the resonance of all previous oak trees has become part of the morphogenetic field, and that resonance influences and dictates the essential form of each new oak as it develops. The acorn is, as it were, surrounded by an oak tree field, which ultimately ensures that oak trees all share similar characteristics.[2] Sheldrake points out that if one removes the cells that normally develop into particular organs in a biological form, other cells will take over the functions of the absent cells, as though there were some overarching plan for the finished structure being followed by the organism as a whole. Sheldrake speaks of the stable characteristics exhibited by any form as "habits". Where human behaviors are concerned, he pictures the psyche as a kind of radio receiver that "tunes in" to resonance patterns in the morphogenetic field. Collective memory, in this view, is not located in the psyche of the individual, but exists as a repository of patterns available to the psyche. Memory in this sense partakes of teleology.

Of course, Sheldrake's ideas about archetypal form quite nearly stand Jung's ideas on their head. Jung postulated the stability of collective potential and malleability of individual form. Sheldrake postulates the malleability of collective potential and the stability of individual form. This is an interesting distinction. When a Jungian discusses therapy as an archetypal configuration of elements, she or he means that the form and behaviors involved share collective ground with other kinds of ritualized healing dyads cross-culturally, because all derive from a common psychological impetus. Sheldrake's point of view suggests something different: it suggests that the therapeutic system—its structure, form and process—has inherent properties determined by the morphogenetic resonance built up by all such preceeding forms. The psyches of patient and therapist are "tuning in" to a pattern of resonance that, in a sense, mandates the kind of relationship that occurs.

This point of view would suggest that clinicians and theorists have not participated so much in the evolution of the essential elements of treatment (the basic therapeutic format and the various psychic processes held to occur in a successful therapy), but in the recognition of elements inherent in the form, which are set in motion by the resonance of a therapeutic pattern in the morphogenetic field. In other words, the archetypal form of the therapeutic system dictates particular kinds of psychological experience, as determined by the form taken by therapeutic rites across time and culture for millennia.

Elementary Particles and the Quantum Field Theory

One can also look at this idea from the point of view of physics. With progressively advanced technology, science has discovered, discarded, and discovered anew answers to the question of what constitutes the primary element of material existence. Each element heralded as primary proved ultimately to be constituted itself of elements more primary. Even the atom, once presumed the primary building block of all matter, lost its claim to electrons, protons, and neutrons, the so-called elementary particles.

On the basis of this latter finding, research was mounted in particle physics, and the results have since mandated a point of view that has revolutionized science. As Zukav (1979) explains, experiments were initially designed in terms of traditional expectations: Particles were shot at one another in the interest of determining which elements survived. These basic elements would then be presumed to be "the ultimate building blocks of the universe" (p. 214).

What happened, however, forced science to another vantage point on what is popularly understood as reality. Zukav writes:

> *When the projectile strikes the target, both particles are destroyed at the point of impact. In their place, however, are created new particles all of which are as elementary as the original particles and often as massive as the original particles...[in other words, every] subatomic interaction consists of the annihilation of the original particle and the creation of new subatomic particles. (p. 215)*

In constructing a theory of creation based on these discoveries, quantum field theory postulates that:

Fields alone are real. They are the substance of the universe and not matter. Matter (particles) is simply the momentary manifestations of interacting fields which, intangible and insubstantial as they are, are the only real things in the universe. (p. 219)

Field Theory and the Formation of the Therapeutic Relationship

One might say that this postulate—that form and substance are the properties and byproducts of intangible and insubstantial interacting fields—has made possible Sheldrake's speculations about formative causation. In fact, I would want to read Sheldrake very much in terms of this domain of ideas. Sheldrake's notion of pre-existing patterns can be understood to parallel what physicists are describing as field interactions. In this respect, I would suggest that when applied to processes that evolve over time, morphogenetic resonance can be understood less as a determinant of habitual forms than as a determinant of parameters that dictate probable forms.[3]

This understanding is not only more compatible with Jung's conceptualization of the archetypes, but can serve to render some of Jung's ideas operable in another realm of discourse. Such a translation becomes important when attempting, for example, to discuss the effects of an archetype that appears to be linking individual psyches in the service of a larger collective priority. Quantum theory and its biological derivatives operate from the perspective of the larger field, and require no leap of faith to assume collective effects whose source is the individual mind.

The therapeutic system can be understood in this way as occurring within what might be called a "psychotherapy field". The field is broader than psychotherapy, however; it includes "resonance patterns" built up by all ritual dyads that have been structured for the purpose of healing the psyche. This resonance determines certain parameters that essentially determine what we understand as a patient/therapist relationship. The kind of interchange that occurs in terms of these parameters is, of course, indeterminate; however, its direction may well be predictable probabilistically (Langs, Rapp, Thomson, Pinto, 1988).

The Parameters/Ground Rules of Treatment

In many respects, then, Freud and the pioneers in the domain of psychoanalysis were inventing terms for pieces of a complex mosaic pattern that exists in all relationships that are similarly configured. That is, once patient and therapist enter the therapeutic relationship, a previously established and autonomously determined set of parameters becomes operative, making possible and encouraging particular kinds of responses, conscious and unconscious, in both parties.

Langs's idea that a particular set of conditions are paradigmatic for the successful undertaking of psychotherapy represents an attempt to set back from the evolving process of therapy, and to define the parameters determining its form. It is instructive, in this regard, that Langs has been able to delineate paradigmatic boundary conditions on the basis of his patients' unconscious attempts to establish or to rectify parameters perceived to be absent or mismanaged in the therapeutic relationship. This suggests a psychological analogy to Sheldrake's discussion of cells that take over the functions of other missing cells toward an apparently foreordained structural design. One might say that there is an unconscious paradigm for therapy resident in each patient, whose violation generates responses in terms of individual pathology. Another way of stating this is to say that Langs has been fleshing out the shape of an archetype-a morphogenetic pattern to which individual psyches become attuned under therapeutic circumstances.

One of the important contributions that Langs has made to the field is his recognition that both members of a therapeutic dyad are constantly responding to the stimuli constituted by the experience of therapy itself. By attending to the patient's narratives as the manifest text of his or her unconscious attempts to adapt to the therapeutic experience, the therapist is led to recognize the patient's unconscious response to very specific therapist behaviors. In my own work, I have found that patients do, in fact, unconsciously express their perceptions of the meaning implied by my behaviors; as Langs has pointed out, these implications are worked over in terms of a given patient's emotional fault lines. But patients also generate narratives that reflect issues and events current in my life outside of therapy, particularly issues and events that might be said to share common ground with the emotional difficulties constellated in the treatment. My attempts to link this kind of experience with countertransference could not account for very specific references in patient material to circumstances known only to myself. The idea that therapy in some way liberates telepathic ability is tantalizing, but does not explain why patients are capable of such feats only unconsciously.

On the other hand, if one accepts the idea of a psychotherapy field, one might understand subfields to operate within it. One such subfield is the morphogenetic pattern that stabilizes the personality and behaviors of the therapist. Sheldrake, in fact, insists that each of us constantly "tunes in" to the pattern we have already established for continuity in time and space. This "tuning in" is not accomplished by conscious effort, but seems to be part and parcel of the human system as such. I would suggest that the psychotherapy field determines a form of relationship in which the patient "tunes in" to the therapist's morphogenetic pattern and experiences himself or herself accordingly from a new vantage point.

The Biological Analogy

This relationship of the individual psyche to another field can be understood better, perhaps, in the biological domain. I would maintain that the relationship of the patient's psyche to the therapist's is much like the embryo's to the womb. The patient's psyche becomes embedded in the subfield (morphogenetic resonance patterns) of the therapist, and is, in a sense, reborn from that "womb".

It is clear in the biological domain that the womb-field in which the embryo develops exerts its own influence on the fetus. That is, although the ultimate form of the embryo is determined by its own potential, its development not only depends on the health and capacity of the womb-field to contain it, but also appears to be affected both by the physical and psychological state of the mother. Winnicott (1960) goes so far as to posit the womb-fetus relationship as part of a continuum from which the mother-child proceeds. That is, the developmental process proceeds literally from the biological:

> The mental health of an individual...is laid down by this maternal care, which when it does well, is scarcely noticed, and is a continuation of the physiological provisions that characterizes the prenatal state. This environmental provision is also a continuation of the tissue aliveness and the functional health which (for the infant) provides silent, but vitally important ego support. (p. 47)

One might say that the infant's development is pitched always between the urge to fulfill its own biological, physiological, and spiritual destiny and the constant introjection of the maternal environment. Individuation is partly a matter of sorting out self from non-self, particularly from these aspects of the maternal environment that inhibit development. Again, there is a suggestion that psychological development proceeding from and recapitulating biological development, in that the womb-field, appears to have properties that actually interfere with fetal development, encouraging the fetus to a more complex form of organization. Psychologically, it appears that in moments of extreme interference patterns, the child's unique development is temporarily suspended as it works to metabolize the impact of the interference.

Winnicott's (1960) discussion of the infant's response to these toxic interference patterns is interesting for its resemblance to Langs's idea about the secure therapeutic frame: "The alternative to being is reacting, and reacting interrupts being.... The holding environment therefore has as its main function the reduction to a minimum of impingements to which the infant must react..." (p. 49).

To move this discussion beyond the idea of a biological/ psychological continuum, Erich Neumann (1954) would claim the maternal environment as a kind of root idea in the human psyche. That is, the human experience of development (ontogeny) recapitulates a universal (phylogenetic) ordering. Neumann posits that the human model and experience of the womb stands as a paradigm, the heritage of an earlier form, which itself emerged from an original matrix, the uroboros. He writes: "...all mythology says over and over again that this womb is an image, the woman's womb being only a partial aspect of the primordial" (p. 14).

Reading this against Sheldrake, one might suggest that the resonance of biological form dictates field properties kindred to it in other domains where structure and the need to sort out self from environment constitute a form of ritual rebirth. The patient's psyche becomes embedded in the therapist's psyche, and like the developing embryo, is both influenced by the environmental field and must sort out its own destiny from the interference of that field as it moves toward emergence and individual existence.

CHAPTER 9

CONCLUSION

This book examines the initial interview situation through the presentation of historical, developmental, and clinical material, in an effort to explain why many patients are so acutely sensitive to the conditions of treatment. Secondly, it offers a perspective for interpreting patients' unconscious communication in the first session and the beginning phase of treatment.

Much of the material used for this study highlights patients' unconscious perceptions of the therapeutic relationship and discusses the processes whereby these perceptions are conveyed through derivative, unconscious communication. As I researched this material, I was impressed with the frequency and accuracy of patients' unconscious perceptions about the therapeutic relationship. Patients quickly understood the unconscious implications of certain frame issues and presented these concerns through symbolic unconscious imagery. I had concluded that the strength and accuracy of the patients' perceptions of the harmful aspects of treatment often suggested termination or a fundamental alteration of the existing conditions of treatment.

The second phase of this study required that I question whether I had taken patients' material too literally in assuming their communications actually meant termination. What further complicated this question of viability of the treatment setting was the discovery that patients tended to externalize their internal manic defenses by their acceptance of or requests for special conditions of treatment by the therapist. I have come to realize that analysis is possible under such conditions. What is as important as the analysis of the shared patient and therapist manic defenses is the possible anagogic aspect of the defenses being reconstituted within the analytic vessel. In other words, the recreation of the manic defense processes in treatment could be the psyche's way of creating conditions within which patients can learn about their inner life. A premature termination could represent a rejection of the patient's unconscious attempts to be healed, and could be interpreted as the therapist's introjection (and acting out) of the patient's dread of facing his or her unconscious. An awareness of how patients utilize the conditions of treatment to defend against facing their inner world puts the analyst in an excellent position to begin an in-depth exploration of the patient's unconscious dynamics.

This thesis contributes to the Jungian and Psychoanalytic view of the initial interview in the following ways:

1. It highlights the unconscious communicative network existing between patient and analyst in the initial interview.

2. It reveals that much of patients' communications in the early stages of treatment are veiled references of their unconscious experience of the therapist and the therapeutic setting.

3. It shows that patients' acceptance or requests for special conditions of treatment often represent an externalization of their internal manic defense processes, which will directly affect treatment. If these defenses remain unanalyzed, they could create barriers against effective analytic work, but, if understood, they could

facilitate the patient's understanding of their unconscious dynamics.

4. It demonstrates that Jung's concept of the objective psyche is helpful for understanding the meaning and purpose of patients' communications in the initial interview.

Appendix

Chaotic Attractors in the Therapeutic System[1]

SANDY BERCHULSKI,[†] MICHAEL CONFORTI,[‡] IRENE GUITER-MAZER,[§] and JANE MALONE[ı*]

[†]Psychiatric Clinician at Holyoke Hospital, Holyoke, Massachusetts
[‡]Jungian analyst in private practice, Brattleboro, Vermont Associate Faculty of the Antioch-New England Graduate School, Keene, New Hampshire
[§]Doctoral candidate, Adelphi University, Garden City, New York
[ı*]Therapist at the Monadnock Family Center, Keene, New Hampshire

(Received November 25, 1994; accepted January 10, 1995)

ABSTRACT: Because little research had been done on the presence and role of latent communication in the context of team-conducted family therapy, the writers set out to monitor unconscious responses generated under these conditions. Specifically, they investigated an ongoing family treatment situation conducted according to the "reflecting team model." One team of therapists handles the actual treatment session, while the other observes from behind a one-way mirror. During the course of a session, the second team makes suggestions to the treatment team either by telephone or by calling the therapists out of the treatment room.

As the project developed, the writers found that the unconscious responses of both family and treatment teams indicated a process at work beyond the conscious intentions of the participants. That is, the therapeutic enterprise was functioning as a dynamical system, whose increasing complexity suggested a self organizing principle at work. This paper traces the development of the system's movement toward greater complexity, identifies the specific interventions that indicate this process, describes how all participants demonstrated a high degree of resonance and synchronization with this overarching self organizing pattern. This paper serves to alert therapists to the role of unconscious communication within the therapeutic system and postulates that the generation of form within psychotherapy follows many of the same self organizing processes found in other human and non human systems.

KEYWORDS: chaos theory, perturbation, dynamical systems theory, family therapy, psychoanalytic research, archetypal field theory

The therapist/patient relationship is generally discussed in terms of the inter-personal dynamics generated within it. However, as recent literature in family therapy has demonstrated, the clinical elements of therapy can also be described as a *system*—a bipersonal field determined as much by system parameters as by the psyches of patient and therapist. That is, a therapeutic exchange is created not only by the relationship of the participants, but by the form and structure of the environment in which the dyad is operating, and the form and structure of the communications themselves.

A number of family therapy models have been developed that exploit the systemic approach from differing vantage points. Some of these combine systems theory with object relations theory and so emphasize basic psychoanalytic principles (see, for example, Scharff 1989). Recently, J. Zinner (1989) has applied to family therapy the therapeutic frame theory of psychoanalyst Robert Langs. Zinner's focus, however, is patient-centered and meaning-oriented, as opposed to Langs' own orientation toward structure. It is this structural orientation that dictates the shape of our research. Langs (1978) defines the therapeutic frame as:

> *a metaphor for the implicit and explicit ground rules of psychotherapy or psychoanalysis. The image implies that the ground rules create a basic hold for the therapeutic interaction, and for both patient and therapist, and that they create a distinctive set of conditions within the frame that differentiate it in actuality and functionally from the conditions outside the frame. (p. 632)*

For Langs, the basic condition of the therapeutic relationship is stimulus-and-response adaptation. The specifics of a secure frame are entirely concrete: privacy, confidentiality, consistency of time and place, intervention only to decode unconscious material, no third-party payment, and so forth. He demonstrates through clinical examples (1978, 1982) that deviations from these concrete particulars are expressed unconsciously in the patient's communications. Langs contends, in fact, that these unconsciously expressed perceptions are nontransferential, valid assessments of the adaptive context provided by the therapist. The therapist is obliged to attend to such perceptions by interpretation and, if possible, by rectifying the conditions of treatment.

In other words, the patient's pathology does not distort perception of a stimulus, but does determine which of its implications reach unconscious expression in the therapeutic relationship. Given the therapist's responsibility for frame management, the deviations that reach unconscious expression in the patient's narratives will almost invariably reflect an aspect of shared pathology with the therapist.

Langs's concern with the concrete particulars of the therapeutic enterprise—and with patients' analogical reference to these particulars in narrative communication—has lent itself to the collection of hard data in the clinic, their quantification, and the preliminary construction of a mathematical model for communicative interplay. The goal of Langs's current research is to describe mathematically the substructural order beneath the seemingly arbitrary phenomena of a given session (Langs *et al.* 1988a, 1988b; Rapp *et al.* 1991).

In this respect, his work dovetails very neatly with recent advances in the field of chaos theory. Chaos theory does not regard chaos as a state of confusion and disorder, but as a type of natural randomness that appears in certain biological and physical systems. Indeed, research in the hard sciences has suggested that chaos is actually a form of flexibility—a response to all possible stimuli as opposed to a discriminated response along immediately predictable lines.

More pertinently, the resolution of chaos is not necessarily the restoration of equilibrium, but a potentially higher level of organization, which may be regarded as its purpose. Paul Rapp (1987) has suggested that apparently chaotic neurobiological states—disorders of tremor, dyskinesias, and epilepsy—are actually autonomic corrective mechanisms that re-establish lost neural coordination. In this sense, the seizure is a restorative phenomenon, not a defect, and complex dynamical behavior, or chaos, is an aspect of biological regulation. Equilibrium tends a system toward repetitive behaviors; it renders a system less open to change and less able to respond to new input. Non-equilibrium is the source of order, it brings *"order out of chaos"* (Prigogine and Stengers 1984).

Some of the recent work being undertaken to apply chaos theory to the psychological system was anticipated two generations ago by the Swiss analyst, C. G. Jung. He suggested that the psychotic state is a natural attempt to restore the mind to its normal flexibility. Langs, by concentrating not on the workings of the individual brain, but on the field in which a patient and therapist are embedded, has created a model for examination of a human system rather than a biological or chemical system. His quantification of the variable behaviors and communications that go on in a given session—who is talking, extent of narration, newness of theme, and so forth— has led to research that does in fact suggest a crude form of substructural probability in the therapeutic interaction *(op. cit.).*

We are interested in the macroscopic implications of this work—how a psychological system moves to a far-from-equilibrium state, or chaos, and so gains the ability to evolve toward a higher level of organization.

In a biological system, the movement from equilibrium into non-equilibrium is influenced by several factors. Chemical substances known as catalysts in the system can modify a value, can encourage a system to follow a new reaction path, or can lead it to inhibition. A catalytic effect is the basic condition for the appearance of a far-from-equilibrium state.

If we apply the principles of chaos theory to psychological systems, we need to consider the following points: First, biological systems have a past. Their molecular constitution has evolved to take part in autocatalytic mechanisms that generate very specific forms of organized processes. There is inherent purpose in a system and it seeks to move toward that purpose. This is referred to as deterministic chaos.

Second, the type of fluctuation in the system will lead to the choice of branch the system will follow after the bifurcation point. The system may move to a higher level of organization or to a state of regression, where the chaos is unmetabolized and the system temporarily loses its opportunity to move to greater complexity. The choice, however, cannot be predicted.

Underlying our research was the question: Is there an inherent purpose in a therapeutic system, a deterministic chaos that underlies apparently random events in any given session? What catalyzes a system to move to a higher level of organization or to a state of regression?

Given Langs' preliminary work in this area and his ideas about the patient's unconscious response to the changing stimuli of a system, our research group used his theory as a grounding point. We analyzed a verbatim family session described in *Milan Systemic Family Therapy* (Boscolo *et al.* 1987). This session was a one-time event, conducted to demonstrate the technique of the Milan treatment team. That technique resulted in a varied series of adaptive contexts. Our hypothesis was that the implications of these contexts would be expressed unconsciously in the family's communications as the session progressed. If the therapists did not interpret these unconscious communications, the system would move further and further from equilibrium into a state of chaos. We analyzed the session line by line to determine possible bifurcation points toward either regression or higher organization.

The Milan treatment team consisted of four therapists, Drs. Mara Selvini, Luigi Boscolo, Gianfranco Cecchin, and Guiliana Prata. One male and one female therapist (Cecchin and Selvini) met with the family, while the other two, also a male and a female, observed the session through a one-way mirror. When one of the observing therapists wanted to make an intervention, he or she would knock on the session room door. One of the therapists would exit, listen to the comment, and return to the session. From a Langsian perspective, each disturbance would be considered a frame break and a new adaptive context. Our first task was to notice whether these stimuli were reflected unconsciously in at least some of the patients' narratives.

Our initial strategy in this study was to decode each line of the session for possible meaning of the participants' unconscious communication around these various adaptive contexts. Over the course of a year, each member of our research group individually interpreted the same sections of the session, and all possible interpretations were shared at the next meeting. As we proceeded, we recognized that a notable shift in the conversation of both patients and therapists occurred following Dr. Selvini's first consultation with the observing team. This intervention appeared to be a powerful stimulus, around which a great deal of the remaining interaction was focused. We ultimately decided to look more closely at this one condition of treatment and the unconscious communication that followed.

At the time this session was taking place, the Milan team was undergoing an internal struggle of its own and ultimately broke up. It became clear as we worked our way through the session that Dr. Selvini's leaving the room both expressed the impending split of the team and replicated the dynamics of the family.

Our contention is that this intervention was highly disturbing to the family, but also created a bifurcation point in the treatment, whereby both family and therapists had the opportunity to examine the meaning of their behavior. In other words, we contend that the meaning of this intervention can be determined independently of the intentions and reactions of both patients and therapists. We are drawing here on the findings of deterministic chaos: What appears to be a random disturbance in a system may be substructurally intentional.

The therapeutic system will, as it were, move toward its own resolution, but individual healing will not occur unless the participants become conscious of their mutual participation in the psychodynamic issues involved.

Case Study

As already indicated, the session was conducted to demonstrate the Milan team's technique, which was itself influenced by the work of Gregory Bateson. The team's approach emphasized Bateson's ideas of cybernetic circularity, from which its clinical technique, with its distinctive concepts of hypothesizing, circularity, and neutrality, was derived (Bateson 1988; Boscolo *et al.* 1987). The interview was being taped on closed-circuit television with an audience present. As it happened, the two women in the team were not entirely fluent in English, which was the language of the family. The male team members felt constrained by this handicap. As noted, the treatment team was experiencing tension within its own ranks. Soon after this interview, the two women left the team to begin their own training institute.

The parents of the family had been married five years. Both were divorced and now shared five children (three girls and two boys) from their first marriages. The mother had called to request treatment for her son, John, who had recently spent three weeks on an in-patient psychiatric ward. Diagnosis was an acute schizophrenic attack. The parents were upset that the psychiatrist had not consulted with them. They wondered whether the son's behavior might not have been induced by drug abuse. They also wanted to know if the psychotropic medicine prescribed in the hospital should be continued.

The stated purpose of the Milan team was to clarify the nature of John's problem and to discuss a treatment plan with the clinic. Their pre-hypothesis was based on the mistaken impression that all five children belonged to the mother and that some of the children were allied with the absent natural father. They began the interview with the intention of confirming this pre-hypothesis. As the session progressed, they realized their mistake and modified their questions, attempting to locate the childrens' respective alliances. Their goal was to remove the label of identified patient from John and to portray the family dysfunction as a shared group behavior, not testimony to the illness of one member.

Our literature indicates that the team only later realized the extent to which their own issues were "unconsciously utilized by the family to protect the status quo" (Boscolo *et al.* 1987, p. 32). The dilemma of the team and the dilemma of the family reflected each other in a way that struck one commentator as "quite mysterious" (p. 66). Our analysis of the unconscious communication taking place in this interaction suggests that these similarities were triggered by the interventions of the therapists.

In taking this tack, we believe, with Langs, that the patients' unconscious perceptions of the adaptive context were valid, but selective. We are not seeing in this exchange an example of Freud's compulsion to repeat. We are seeing a confluence between the patients' and therapists' psychological issues, which was expressed unconsciously because of the nature of the therapists' interventions. We propose that this confluence can be usefully explained from the perspective of deterministic chaos.

The therapeutic system may be said to consist of three fields: (1) the internal dynamics of the patient, (2) the therapist, and (3) the interactions of the patient and therapist occurring with the psychotherapy field itself. Our hypothesis invokes the substructural activity of a fourth: the *a priori* laws and regularities that guide the unfolding of the therapeutic relationship. The influence of this latter field on the other three is autonomous—in Jungian terms, archetypal; in Sheldrake's terms, morphogenetic (Jung 1934; Sheldrake 1981).

The decision to call Selvini from the room was a catalyst that ultimately moved the therapeutic system into a state of chaos, portending conscious resolution of the problem and movement to a higher level of organization. In this respect, Selvini's departure may be understood as a chaotic attractor.

In the first part of the interview, the therapist Cecchin did most of the speaking in an attempt to gather information about the family and its dynamics. The responses the family made to his interventions suggest their unconscious perception of the flat and defensive quality of his inquiries. For example, the mother says at one point, "... we've always sat down and had family discussions, and we would sit sometimes for hours talking about nothing." The transcript reads as follows:

123 MOTHER: Well, we've never had any problems.

124 CECCHIN: You said John was a very high-strung boy.

125 FATHER: Well, I'd say "Cut the grass," but he wanted to go

126 out with the boyfriends, so he would prefer to go out with the other

127 kids.

128 MOTHER: He would do it.

129 FATHER: He would do it, but under protest.

130 SELVINI: But you said during the summer he was more cooperative. What

131 about Harry, was he cooperative?

132 MOTHER: Harry's always been good.

133 FATHER: He's always been pretty good.

134 MOTHER: I think they would be normal, if ...

135 FATHER: They're normal kids.

136 SELVINI: Was he more cooperative than John?

137 FATHER: As a rule, yeah.

138 SELVINI: As a rule he's more cooperative.

139 MOTHER: Also, as a rule, we've always sat down and had family discussions,

140 and we would sit sometimes for hours talking about nothing. And

141 John has never really been able to take any type of criticism be it

142 constructive or otherwise, and so he would just leave.

143 CECCHIN: What about the girls? Are they cooperative?

144 MOTHER: They have their moments, the same as I do (laughter).

145 CECCHIN: Who's the less cooperative?

146 FATHER: I wouldn't say the less cooperative, but I'd say the most forgetful

147 would be Donna. If she's going to do something up stairs, she's

148 forgotten what she's supposed to do by the time she gets there.

149 SELVINI: (naming the girls) Barbara, Donna, and Deborah.

150 MOTHER: Barbara's the oldest, then Donna, and then Deborah.

At this point Selvini is called out of the room by the observing team behind the one-way mirror.

151 CECCHIN: Are they cooperative with their father in the same way they're

152 cooperative with their mother?

153 FATHER: I'd say more so.

154 CECCHIN: Who? The girls, you say.

155 FATHER: I don't know.

156 CECCHIN: More so, more cooperative? More cooperative with you?

157 FATHER Well, yeah. If I say do it, they usually do it.

The family laughs and jokes with Cecchin. Selvini comes back in.

Analysis

Our analysis of the presence and effect of chaotic attractors in this consultation sequence focuses on the patients' unconscious responses to the therapists' interventions. Noteworthy is the fact that Selvini was called out of the room in the middle of a discussion about the cooperation of the boys versus the girls in the family. Recall that the treatment team eventually broke up along gender-lines over tensions of this sort in their own ranks. Immediately preceding this discussion are the lines to which we alluded earlier, 139 to 142. After Cecchin's inquiries about the family's background, mother says that the family often sat for hours talking about nothing. This is a very clear reflection of her unconscious perceptions of Cecchin's interventions. From the standpoint of chaos theory, she is describing a near-equilibrium state that lacks the energic charge of high perturbation. The meaninglessness of the exchange matches the meaninglessness that prevails in the family.

Mother then speaks of people who are unable to hear criticism and who just leave the room. Cecchin immediately shifts the subject and introduces an arbitrary division between the sons and daughters. The mother responds by aligning herself with the daughters, and the father makes a new reference to someone leaving the room: He says one of the daughters will go upstairs to get something, then forget why she went. Selvini reaffirms the gender division initiated by Cecchin. She states the names of the three daughters and is echoed by mother. At that point Selvini is called from the room.

Boscolo, the male observer who summoned Selvini from the room, explained his reasons for doing so:

We wanted to discuss with her the idea of putting an explanatory question to the family, to ask them to give their hypotheses about John's behavior. With somebody this upset, especially when he is so heavily labeled, the family doesn't give much information. They tend either to be tangential or else they give the opinion of the experts, the doctors. This family gives us feedback they got from the doctors as you see. If you ask for a hypothesis, you introduce a possible connection between them and the one who is sick. There is the possibility that they will reveal themselves. This can make family members very anxious. (Boscolo et al 1987, p. 47)

Our own conclusions are based on the unconscious valence of the patient-therapist exchange. The therapists, unable to appreciate the unconsciously expressed references to their work as nonproductive *("talking about nothing")* responded behaviorally to the underlying meaning of the family's communications. Cecchin ignored the mother's mention of someone leaving the room because of confrontation and criticism, but he responded in a way that reflected his own problems with criticism on the team and the impending departure of the two female members. The division along gender lines, which Cecchin unconsciously read into the family's dynamics, was echoed by Selvini, at which point Boscolo, the male member of the observing team, called her out of the room. We can see in his rationale the team's unconscious awareness of the expanding disequilibrium in the system. Boscolo's stated intention was to instruct Selvini to return to the very mode of questioning the mother had unconsciously defined as nonproductive—the equilibrium state.

Yet, as it turned out, his decision to pull Selvini from the room served, instead, as a chaotic attractor. It created a state of disturbance that might have drawn the system toward higher complexity, had the participants been aware of the opportunity. To put this another way, the family's unconscious communications perturbated the system enough to force the team into making a pivotal intervention. By pivotal we do not mean that the intervention was appropriate; we mean that the intervention was all but instinctive, notwithstanding the expressed rationale of the performers—part of the system's own teleological movement toward higher complexity.

When Selvini returned, she attempted to initiate the line of questioning Boscolo had advised her to pursue:

162 SELVINI: I want to ask: When John began this behavior two days before

163 school, what was the explanation you gave for this behavior?

164 When you tried to find out...

165 FATHER: No, the kids knew, they didn't tell us. We didn't notice it until

166 the day after he went to school, but the kids are starting to tell

167 us these things happened a few days before, but didn't tell us.

168 BARBARA: We didn't think nothing happened until (name of boyfriend) told

169 us that John was having a nervous breakdown.

170 SELVINI: What was the explanation you gave for this behavior of John's?

171 FATHER: We didn't know. We took him right to the doctor. We talked to him

172 and we knew, obviously, that he had a problem we couldn't cope

173 with, so we took him down to emergency in the hospital and had the

174 doctor check him.

175 SELVINI: But commonly in the family, they try to find some explanation for

176 this sort of behavior, why. . .

177 FATHER: What we first suspected was possibly drugs.

178 MOTHER: That was our first, you know——

179 FATHER: I mean, we didn't know; that's the first thing you think of. So

180 the doctor checked him and he said there was no evidence of

181 anything being taken.

182 MOTHER: But then later on he said that during the summertime, when he was

183 on vacation for a week, that the boys had tried some LSD, so

184 we thought maybe he'd had a recurrence, and it was very confusing

185 because the psychiatrist—we couldn't speak to him. And I was

186 trying to figure out whether you differentiate an acid trip from

187 a schizophrenic episode. And the doctor said, "Oh yes, definitely,

188 he was having a schizophrenic episode." Later on, he said he

189 didn't think he was schizophrenic, and I said, "Are there any

190 tests to determine yes or no?" And he said, "No, there aren't."

191 So then my husband and I came to the clinic because we saw an ad

192 in the paper, and then we asked one of the doctors here if it could

193 be confirmed one way or the other. And he said yes. So then I went

194 back to the doctor and I said, "Could we take him up to the clinic

195 to have him assessed?" And he said, "Well, yes, but you won't find

196 out anything more than you know now." And I said, "I want to find

197 out one way or the other," and he said, "Oh, yes, definitely

198 schizophrenic." He said, "You were there, you saw all the

199 symptoms."

200 CECCHIN: Did you find out if he took LSD or not during the summer?

201 MOTHER: He says he didn't.

202 CECCHIN: Anybody else in the family try drugs? (Children laugh.) LSD? At

203 the same time he took it?

204 HARRY: Yeah.

205 CECCHIN: (to John) Did you have some strange effects?

206 JOHN: No, didn't have any side effects.

207 CECCHIN: From what you understand, is there any relation between LSD and

208 what happened to you?

209 JOHN: No.

210 CECCHIN: There's no relation? What's your explanation of what happened to

211 you?

212 JOHN: I don't know.

213 CECCHIN: You said something to your sister, "I have something to say, but I

214 cannot say it," so you must have something on your mind.

215 JOHN: I know, but ...

216 CECCHIN: You forgot or you couldn't say?

217 JOHN: I don't know.

218 CECCHIN: Even now you don't know. Whom do you talk to in the family when

219 you have a problem?

220 JOHN: Everybody.

221 CECCHIN: Anybody special?

222 JOHN: (starting to cry) No, just anybody—Barbara, Harry, Donna.

Analysis

In this section, Selvini moves to focus the attention on the family and the behavior of one of its members. Again, the mother delivers the brunt of the family's unconscious perceptions of the adaptive context. Following a number of references from other family members to John's strange behavior and possible drug use, she speaks of information being withheld, doctors' reluctance to help the family, psychosis, and so forth. The high incidence of images about disturbed functioning from all the members can be taken as the family's unconscious experience of this treatment environment. The mother specifically mentions a doctor who seemed to withhold the correct diagnosis and said there was no way to make a diagnosis. Again, Cecchin shifts the subject, then directs increasingly aggressive and accusing questions at John about his drug experiences. Recall, here, that the team's stated goal was to portray the family's dysfunction as a group phenomenon and to remove the identified patient label from John. The effect of Cecchin's questioning is ultimately to break John down.

At this point in the treatment, the family's dynamics are entirely paralleled by those of the treatment team. All members of this enterprise are now embedded in a psychotic field. We quote again from the commentary on this particular case, and the attempt of Lynn Hoffman, a family therapist and an authority in systems theory, to address this phenomenon:

It is really quite mysterious how those events take place, how the dilemma of the team and the dilemma of the family reflect each other. For instance, all morning we've been talking about the lack of confirmation for the two young males in this family while at the same time, we see that the two men on the team feel they must restrain their effectiveness to keep in sync with the rules of their team (Boscolo *et al.* 1987, p. 66)

Although Hoffman clearly recognizes that something interesting is occurring within the therapeutic system, she lacks a theory to explain it. Our theory is that such phenomena are governed by a set of laws or regularities that orchestrate the system toward a particular end.

Deterministic Chaos and the Role of a Chaotic Attractor in this Session

Until the observing team called Selvini from the room, the therapeutic system was operating in a relatively dysfunctional manner, but the degree of dysfunction was syntonic to the family. The family expressed its unconscious perceptions and experience of the consultation, but the team members were unable to understand the communications and in fact reacted unconsciously to defend themselves from their implications. These perturbations were small enough so that the evolution of the system remained regular, if somewhat distorted. According to Jensen, "... the perturbation must become rather large before the evolution of a single phase trajectory begins..." (Jensen 1987, p. 174).

We can see evidence of increasing disequilibrium just before Selvini left. Although other chaotic attractors may be discerned or conjectured in this session, Selvini's departure was the one that was strong enough to move the system. It also served as an opportunity to elucidate the meaning of the session and, in turn, the family dynamics. In this light, this moment was a chaotic attractor that drew the available energy within the field to it.

As the work of Prigogine and Laszlo suggest, in the presence of a strong perturbation, a system is forced into a position of reorganization (Prigogine and Stengers 1984; Laszlo 1987).

This developmental process is defined by Prigogine as *"evolutionary feedback."* To quote Hoffman,

> *"[Evolutionary feedback] means that a movement that is only a fluctuation in a system at one time can suddenly become the basis for an entirely new arrangement of the system at another time." (Hoffman 1981, p. 340)*

In this consultation, a major byproduct of the observing team's intervention in the therapeutic process was the revealed alliance between John and Selvini. Both served as identified patients in their respective fields. One might suggest that deterministic chaos actually *requires a* resonance between therapist and patient for its activation and mobilization. Recall Langs's idea that a patient will actively, if unconsciously, seek out a therapist whose *"madness"* matches his or her own (Langs 1987).

Rupert Sheldrake (1981,1988) has posited in the field of biology the existence of a *"resonance field,"* which determines the unfolding of a particular morphogenetic pattern. For example, an acorn has no chemical blueprint or mechanism that determines its morphological destiny as an oak, yet it follows a very specific pattern of unfolding into a particular kind of tree. Sheldrake finds evidence for the existence of a *"morphogenetic field"*—an oak-tree field—that determines the development of any given acorn into an oak tree.

All new life, whether a fetus in the womb or a patient in psychotherapy, gestates within a field. The conditions of the field clearly influence the evolution of the developing life contained within it. From this perspective, life can be viewed as an organism's response to its environment and the carrying out of prefigured regularities within it.

Discussing the possible meaning for the appearance of disability and the regularities occurring within human nature, Jung writes:

> *... neurotic symptoms and complexes are also elaborate "arrangements" which inexorably pursue their aims, with incredible*

obstinancy and cunning. Neurosis is teleologically oriented. (Jung 1953, p. 40)

Although not explicit in his work, Langs's ideas about the therapeutic field rests on a set of similar assumptions. Langs stresses the importance of the therapeutic frame and develops a type of field theory with properties that are evident in the regularity of patients' responses to conditions of treatment. By turning the lens of modern physics and systems theory to the therapeutic situation, we can posit that much of what occurs in treatment represents an unfolding of a set of innate laws and regularities (Bohm 1980).

Our study demonstrates a moment of development in one particular field. The resonance between team and family was the direct result of the therapists' inability to recognize their own contribution to the meaning system created by the family's distress. As the system moved into a far-from-equilibrium state, or chaos, the resonance created a matrix out of which evolution of the entire system could potentially occur. Selvini's leaving is an example of the system's self-organizing property. The attempted process or reorganization occurred beyond the conscious recognition of the members within the system.

We are suggesting here that a system's own set of laws may have a pivotal role in forcing certain clinical interventions. One may question the validity of the team's therapeutic plan in this family session, but one cannot ignore the effect their interventions ultimately had on the evolution of the system.

Undoubtedly, the question of teleology and the concept of deterministic chaos are difficult to entertain from a mechanistic/linear perspective. Non-linear dynamics views chaos as a natural phase of a system's growth essential for its evolution into higher forms of organization. If we accept the latter point of view, we would be obliged to see a therapist's mistaken intervention not merely as an aberration of sound treatment, but as part and parcel of an evolutionary development toward higher complexity. Management of chaotic interactive patterns in a therapeutic system would lie in the clinician's ability to interpret their meaning after the fact. This is not easy business. A clinician must stand ready to accept his or her own unconscious portion in a resonance field. Here we stand with Langs: Interpretation of expressed unconscious perceptions of the system is essential.

In many of the cases we have examined, there is a high incidence of confluence between the patient's disabilities and the frame construction and deviations in the treatment environment. Patients appear to seek out clinical settings that in some accurate and at times uncanny way parallel their internal issues. As we have indicated, Langs often refers to this phenomenon, but believes it to exist as a kind of *folie de deux*. We would maintain that such attempted repetition of a complex in a congenial environment is less evidence of an arrested state of psychological development than of the patient's embeddedness in a certain field. The laws and regularities of that field will determine the patient's behavior until he or she develops some degree of insight and resolves the original problem. This near-equilibrium state requires a chaotic attractor to move it to a level of new complexity.

As we have seen in the session just described, the unconscious resonance between a patient and therapist can result in disturbances that ultimately push the system to autonomous self-correction. A chaotic attractor is activated, which functions as a kind of irritant, mobilizing the system to a far-from-equilibrium state and the potential for reorganization. One might think of the sand that mobilizes an oyster's resources into metabolizing the irritant, thus creating a pearl.

In our particular session, the clinicians did not address the unconscious dynamics of the system's move toward chaos, and there was no way to metabolize its meaning. An emphasis on destruction and hopelessness set in and were expressed in images of violence and poor functioning.

Conclusion

Our research would appear to suggest that just as the conscious mind is moved by unconscious intentionality, the unconscious mind is moved by the very archetype of order. Cognition, intention, and the will, those reigning totems of consciousness, must co-exist with an ordering principle that lies outside the domain of personal dynamics. Its existence may well express itself in events that can be analyzed and understood only in retrospect.

As psychologists and investigators, we are not in a position to speak of transcendent meaning, but from a systemic point of view, it might be said that the events of living systems are important not in and of themselves, but for the evolution they make possible. The changes that occur in our lives are not random; they are part of a larger pattern, to which, given the evidence of sessions like this one, we are very often blind. We need to shift in our thinking about the world as well as the therapeutic enterprise.

References

Bateson, G. 1988. *Steps to an Ecology of Mind* Northvale, NJ: Jason Aronson, Inc.

Bohm, D. 1980. *Wholeness and the Implicate Order.* New York: Routledge & Kegan Paul, Ltd.

Boscolo, L., Checchin, G., Hoffman, L., and Penn, P. 1987. *Milan Systemic Family Therapy.* New York: Basic Books.

Hoffman, L. 1981. *Foundations in Family Therapy.* New York: Basic Books.

Jensen, R. 1987. Classical chaos. *American Scientist,* (March-April), 168-181.

Jung, C. G. 1934. Archetypes of the Collective Unconscious. In Adler, G., Fordham, M., and Read, H.

(eds.) : *The Collected Works of C. G. Jung,* Vol. 9, 1., translated by R. F. C. Hull. New York and Princeton

(Bollingen Series XX) and London, 1954.

Jung, C. G. 1953. The Other Point of View. In Adler, G., Fordham, M., and Read, H. (eds.): *The Collected Works of C. G. Jung, Vol.* 7, translated by R. F. C. Hull. New York and Princeton (Bollingen Series XX) and London, 1954.

Langs, R. 1978. *The Listening Process.* NJ: Jason Aronson, Inc.

Langs, R. 1982. *Psychotherapy: A Basic Text.* New York: Aronson.

Langs, R. 1987. *A Primer of Psychotherapy.* New York: Gardner Press.

Langs, R. J., Bucci, W., Bryant, R., Ferguson, R., and Thomson, L. 1988a. Two Methods of Quantitatively

Assessing Unconscious Communication in Psychotherapy. Presented at the 1988 Annual Meeting of

The Society for Psychoanalytic Psychotherapy, New York, New York.

Langs, R. J., Rapp, P. E., Thomson, L., and Pinto, A. 1988b. A Method for Quantifying the Therapeutic

Process: Themes of Gender and Identity. Technical Report Center for Communicative Research,

Beth Israel Hospital, New York, New York.

Laszlo, E. 1987. *Evolution: The Grand Synthesis.* Boston: Shambhala Publications.

Prigogine, I., and Stengers, 1. 1984. *Order Out of Chaos: Man's New Dialogue with Nature.* New York: Bantam Books.

Rapp, P. E., Albano, A., deGuzman, G., and Mees, A.1.1987. Data Requirements for Reliable Estimation of Correlation Dimensions. In Holden, A. V. (ed.): *Chaotic Biological Systems.* New York: Pergamon Press.

Rapp, P. E., Jimenez-Montano, M. A., Langs, R. J., Thomson, L., and Mees, A. 1. 1991. Toward a Quantitative

Characterization of Patient-Therapist Communication. *Mathematical Biosciences,* 105, 207-227.

Scharff, J. 1989. *Foundations of Object Relations Family Therapy.* Northvale, NJ: Jason Aronson, Inc.

Sheldrake, R 1981. *A New Science of Life: The Hypothesis of Formative Causation.* Los Angeles: J. P. Tarcher, Inc.

Sheldrake, R 1988. *The Presence of the Past.* London: Collins.

Zinner, J. 1989. The Use of Concurrent Therapies: Therapeutic Strategy of Re-enactment. In: Scharff, J.

(ed): *Foundations of Qbject Relations family Therapy.* Northvale, NJ: Jason Aronson, Inc.

End Notes

Notes by Chapter

Chapter 3 Notes

[1] I have extended this idea and now frame this entire issue as a field phenomenon. The field in which the child is cared for is made up of the parents' attitudes at time of conception and their behavior and care for child during the beginning phase of life.

[2] When this paper was written, I tended to consider frame related issues as either healthy or disruptive. I have since expanded this view, and now see the actual enactment in the patient/therapist relationship as a recapitulation of powerful personal and archetypal dynamics operative within the lives of both parties. In this regard, the actual so-called frame breaks may be seen not only as potentially disruptive, but also as highly expressive and illustrative of these dynamics, which need to be understood. This insight helped significantly to shift my perception away from viewing pathology as an important shaper of human experience, to seeing expression as the central driver. In no way is this meant to minimize the importance of frame-related issues. Rather it recommends a more rigorous approach,

and a need to understand the specific nature of the enactment occurring between patient and therapist.

³ In time I came to also see it was not so much the therapist's field, as a truly bi-personal, interactive, unified field. In this regard, we begin to find that the actions occurring within the field, whether taken on by patient or therapist, are actions of the field itself, utilizing either member of therapeutic dyad to portray the archetype constellated in the treatment.

⁴ This term, developed by Robert Langs, is in many ways a precursor to much of the work I have been doing since this original study, in viewing not only the therapeutic setting but all interactive dynamics as part of a larger field. Langs's idea of a bi-personal field has served an important role in bridging general and dynamical systems theory and my work on field theory to the therapeutic situation and to life itself. This is especially important in the field of psychotherapy. While virtually every clinician will espouse a theory of patient-therapist interactions, we find interpretive activity in virtually every instance focusing solely about the patient's dynamics, overlooking the fact that the dynamics occurring in the patient/therapist dyad are part of a much larger field.

CHAPTER 4 NOTES

¹ It is interesting to note that Jung's pioneering study of the correspondence between complexes and their physiological responses anticipated not only psychosomatic studies, but also the recent correlation between matter-psyche studies and the emerging field of mind-body psychology.

² While maladaptive in terms of generative behavior, the patient's activities are aligned to the core of the complex. Any tendencies, thoughts, and behaviors are in fact those of the complex itself. For a detailed discussion of this theme, see my book, *Field, Form and Fate: Patterns in Mind, Nature and Psyche.*

³ The use of the word "confessed" is confusing because it infers there was conscious intent to conceal information. Jung's point

was that following the interpretation of his responses to the Association Test, the patient suddenly became aware of what occurred on the previous night, and the repression of the unconscious truth evaporated.

[4] Though the patient's associations revealed an event from his personal experiences, an argument can be made against my use of the term objective psyche. I am using this term to describe the truth-rendering aspects of unconscious functioning, and believe that anything enabling the individual to face his personal truth is related to Self. Also, in the clinical section of this book I show the relationship between personal and archetypal levels of a patient's communication.

[5] Definition taken from C.L. Barnhart & J. Stein, Eds. *The American Heritage Dictionary*, New York: Random House. 1963, p. 950.

[6] In *Field, Form and Fate*, I extend these ideas through a discussion of the term *entrainment*, a word which is used to describe the creation of resonance between seemingly disconnected elements. The idea is taken from the fields of engineering and harmonics.

[8] Since writing this thesis, I have arrived at a new position regarding defenses, denial, etc., and now realize that it is not so much that the client is avoiding the issue, as they are repeating the prior experience. In this regard, the past is not only made present, but the field, which was initiated by the past events, is as powerful a shaper of experience in the current life as it had been in the past.

[9] For further discussion of this concept, see my book *Field, Form and Fate: Patterns in Mind, Nature & Psyche,*

CHAPTER 5 NOTES

[1] For more on Jung's clinical work, I refer the reader to *Jung: A Biography* by Deirdre Bair.

² Brome mentions that Jung suffered from eczema during his childhood, and that it erupted during periods of unrest within his family. This fact might have been another influence affecting his reactions to the patient.

³ The activities occurring within this patient/therapist field can be viewed as the operations of a unified field constellated between them, into which both entered during these interviews.

CHAPTER 6 NOTES

¹ Comment by Yoram Kaufman, C. G. Jung Institute, New York, Spring 1985.

CHAPTER 7 NOTES

¹ For a detailed discussion of this topic see Robert Lang's *The Evolution of the Emotion-processing Mind: With an Introduction to Mental Darwinism*. London: Karnac Books, 1996 and *Psychotherapy and Science*. London: Sage Publications, 1999.

² Since writing this book I have developed a deep and ongoing interest in the effects of such replicative patterns, and the ways in which issues from the lives of both patient and therapist find their way into the therapeutic relationship in the form of some type of reenactment. I have found the following resources immensely valuable in both assessing these situations and learning more about their dynamics: Edward Whitmont's *The Alchemy of Healing*, on the general field of homeopathic cure; D'Arcy Thompson's *On Growth and Form*; and Vilmos Csanyi's work on replicative systems. Each speaks to the workings of a stable morphogenetic/form-shaping field, which works to conserve the given form in any organism or system. Such is the case in patient-therapist dynamics.

Chapter 8 Notes

[1] I am grateful to Lenore Thompson Bentz for editing this section of my thesis. This chapter represents my initial inquiries into the relationship between the new sciences and Jungian psychology, especially with the science of emergence. My inclusion of the theory of morphogenesis and morphogentic dynamics represents my early attempts to understand those form shaping influences inherent within the natural world and human psyche. Rupert Sheldrake's *A New Science of Life: The Hypothesis of Morphic Resonance* was instrumental in my thinking through this material, and I hope my extension of this work, by bringing in the archetypal dimensions of form, has made some contribution to this field.

[2] The image of the acorn is compelling, and has motivated many authors to look at this as a way of understanding the inception of form from preformed fields. Interestingly enough, not only James Hillman's *The Soul's Code* drew extensively on this image, but also my book *Field, Form and Fate* also drew on this image as an entrée into the world of *a priori* form.

[3] I want to thank my friend and colleague, Dr. Fred Abraham, for the many discussions and insights he has shared about the workings and developments of fields. Of particular importance is a statement he made in his 2006 Assisi Institute lecture on initial conditions: "Systems develop their own trajectories, and these trajectories are expressions of the attractor sites which govern the development of the system." In this regard we can see the correlation between fields and archetypes, in that each generates its own phenomena. We also can begin to see form as both intrinsic to, and an epiphenomenon of, the field-archetype itself.

CHAPTER 10 NOTES

[1] Similar to Chapter 8, "Morphogenetic Dynamics in the Analytic Relationship", this chapter represents an important bridge into the domain of matter/psyche studies, which has been the central focus of my interest for the past twenty years. The ideas in this chapter draw from the workings of chaos theory. and were perhaps the most pivotal discoveries and insights that enabled my transition from viewing patient/therapist reenactments as being for the sole purpose of creating madness to viewing these interactions from the perspective of an unconscious and innate ordering process striving to create new order.

In this paper I describe these therapeutic interactions as generated by chaotic attractors. In retrospect I can now see that the occurrences were generated by stable and fixed attractors that govern the trajectories of the patient/therapist interaction, so that they remained within a certain fixed orbit. In other words, the stable attractor maintaining the system was just tha—stable,from the point of view of sharing each other's habitual problems.

Also, I now see that the workings of these stable attractors resulted in a high degree of fidelity to replicative/iterative dynamic. This concept is the basis of my book *Field, Form and Fate: Patterns in Mind, Nature & Psyche*.

While not part of the original dissertation, I felt it was essential to include this piece for the purpose of showing the evolution of my thought in this area.

(Originally presented at the 1989 annual meeting of The Society for Psychoanalytic Psychotherapy, New York, New York.)

REFERENCES

Alexander, I. (1982). The Freud-Jung relationship—the other side of Oedipus and countertransference: Some implications for psychoanalytic theory and psychotherapy. *The American Psychologist, 9,* 1009-1018.

Beres, D. & Obers, S. (1950). The effects of extreme deprivation in infancy on psychic structure in adolescence: A study of ego development. In R.S. Eissler (Ed.), *The Psychoanalytic Study of the Child: Vol. 5.* New York: International University Press,

Barnhart, C.L. & Stein, J. (1963). The American Heritage Dictionary. New York: Random House.

Blomeyer, R. (1980). Children's drawings during first interviews and their unconscious relationship to the investigator. In I. Baker (Ed.), *Methods of Treatment in Analytical Psychology.* Stuttgart: Bonz Verlag.

Briffault, R. (1927). *The Mothers: A Study of the Origins of Sentiments and Institutions.* New York: Macmillian Co.

Brome, V. (1978). *Jung.* New York: Atheneum.

Cirlot, J. E. (1962). *A Dictionary of Symbols.* New York: Philosophical Library.

Deutsch, F., & Murphy, W. (1955a). *The Clinical Interview: Volume I - Diagnosis.* New York: International University Press.

_____. (1955b). *The Clinical Interview: Volume II - Therapy.* New York: International University Press.

Eliade, M. (1964). *Shamanism: Archaic Techniques of Ecstasy.* NJ: Princeton University Press.

Ferenczi, S. (1926). *Further Contributions to the Theory and Practice of Psychoanalysis.* London: Hogarth Press.

Fordham, M. (1976). *The Self and Autism.* London: William Heinemann Medical Books.

Freud, S. (1912). Recommendations to physicians practicing psychoanalysis. *Standard Edition 12:111-120.* London: Hogarth Press, 1958.

_____. (1913). On beginning the treatment. (Further recommendations on the technique of psychoanalysis). *Standard Edition 12:121-144.* London: Hogarth Press, 1958.

_____. (1915a). Beyond the pleasure principle. *Standard Edition 18: 7-64.* London: Hogarth Press,1955.

_____. (1915b). Repression. *Standard Edition. 14:143-158.* London: Hogarth Presss, 1957.

_____. (1915c). Communications between the two systems. *Standard Edition. 14:190-195.* London: Hogarth Press,1957.

Goodheart,W. (1984a). C.G. Jung's first patient: on the seminal emergence of Jung's thought. *Journal of Analytical Psychology. 29:1-34.*

_____. (1984b). Successful and unsuccessful interventions in Jungian analysis: The construction and destruction of the spellbinding circle. In N. Schwartz-Salant and M. Stein, (Eds.), *Transference/Countertransference.* Wilmette, IL: Chiron, 1984.

Goodwin, B.C. (1972). Biology and meaning. In C.H. Waddington (Ed.), *Towards a Theoretical Biology.* London: Edinburgh University Press.

_____. (1978). A cognitive view of biological process. In *Journal of Biological Structures, Vol. 1,* 1978, pp. 117-125.

_____. (1989). Organisms and minds as dynamic forms. *Leonardo, Vol. 22, No.1.* pp. 27-31.

_____. (1986). A science of qualities. In Hiley, B. (ed.), *Quantum Implications.* London: Routledge & Kegan Paul, 1987, pp. 1-23.

Greenacre, P. (1952). *Trauma, Growth and Personality.* New York: W.W. Norton & Company, Inc.

Guggenbuhl-Craig, A. (1976). *Power in the Helping Professions.* New York: Putnam Books.

Harlow, H. (1962). The heterosexual affectional system in monkeys. *American Psychologist, Vol. 17,* pp. 1-9.

Jung, C.G. (1916). General aspects of dream interpretation. *Collected Works, Vol 8: 237-280.*

NJ: Princeton University Press, 1960.

_____. (1937). Psychology and religion: The autonomy of the unconscious. *Collected Works, Vol. 11: 5-105.* NJ: Princeton University Press, 1958.

_____. (1946). Psychology of the transference. *Collected Works, Vol. 16: 164-320.* NJ: Princeton University Press, 1954.

_____. (1950). Concerning Mandala Symbolism. *Collected Works, Vol. 9.1.* NJ: Princeton University Pres.

_____. (1953). Psychology and alchemy. *Collected Works, Vol 16.* NJ: Princeton Univeristy Press.

_____. (1956). Symbols of transformation. *Collected Works, Vol. 5.* NJ: Princeton University Press.

_____. (1957). Psychiatric activities. *Collected Works, Vol 1.* NJ: Princeton University Press.

_____. (1960). Psycholgical types. *Collected Works, Vol. 6.* NJ: Princeton University Press.

_____. (1962). *Memories, Dreams, Reflections.* NY: Pantheon Books.

_____. (1963). Mysterium coniunctionis. *Collected Works, Vol 14.* NJ: Princeton University Press.

_____. (1967). Alchemical studies. *Collected Works, Vol. 13.* NJ: Princeton University Press.

Kerenyi, C. (1947). *Asklepios: Archetypal Image of the Physician's Existence.* New York: Pantheon Books.

Klein, M. (1961). *Narrative of a Child Analysis: The Conduct of the Psychoanalysis of Children as Seen in the Treatment of a Ten Year Old Boy.* New York: Dell Publishing Co.

Kohut, H. (1971). *The Analysis of the Self: A Systemic Approach to the Psychoanalytic Treatment of Narcissistic Personality Disorders.* New York: International University Press.

Langs, R. (1975). The therapeutic relationship and deviations in technique. In *International Journal of Psychoanalytic Psychotherapy.* 4:106-141.

_____. (1982). *Psychotherapy: A Basic Text.* New York: Aronson.

_____. (1984). Making interpretations and securing the frame: sources of danger for psychotherapists. In *International Journal of Psychoanalytic Psychotherapy,* 10: 3-23. New York: Jason Aronson.

_____. (1984). The first session. *The Yearbook of Psychoanalytic Psychotherapy* 1:125-150. NJ: Newconcept Press.

Langs, R., Rapp, P.E., Thomson, L., & Pinto, A. (1988). A method for quantifying the therapeutic process: themes of gender and identity. Unpublished.

Laszlo, E. (1987). *Evolution:The Grand Synthesis.* Boston: Shambhala Publications.

_____. (1988). *Evolution, the Cosmic Dimension: Introduction to the PSI Field Hypothesis.* Boston:Shambhala Publications.

Little, M. (1981). *Transference Neurosis and Transference Psychosis*. New York: Jason Aronson, Inc.

Lubetski, Meir (Ed.) (2002). *Saul Lieberman (1898 - 1983) Talmudic Scholar and Classicist*. NY: Edwin Mellen Press.

Mahler, M. (1968). *On Human Symbiosis and the Vicissitudes of Individuation*. New York: International University Press.

Majno, G. (1975). *The Healing Hand: Man and Wound in the Ancient World*. Massachusetts: Harvard University Press.

Masson, J. (1984). "Freud and the Seduction Theory: A Challenge to the Foundations of Psychoanalysis." *Atlantic Monthly*. (February 1984), pp. 33-60.

McCurdy, A. (1982). Establishing and maintaining the analytic structure. In M. Stein (Ed.), *Jungian Analysis*. Ill: Open Court Publishing Company, 1982, pp. 47-67.

Meier, C. (1967). *Ancient Incubation and Modern Psychotherapy*. Evanston: Northwestern University Press.

Miller, A. (1981). *Prisoners of Childhood: The Drama of the Gifted Child and the Search for the True Self*. New York: Basic Books, 1981.

Mindel, A. (1973). The psychoid nature of the transference. *Quadrant 14*: 5-16.

Morgan, R. (1983). *The Iatrogenics Handbook*. Toronto: IPI Publishing Limited.

Morris, R. (1983). *Evolution and Human Nature*. New York: Seaview/Putnam.

Neumann, E. (1954). *Origins and History of Consciousness*. NJ: Princeton University Press.

_____. (1955). *The Great Mother: An Analysis of the Archetype*. NJ: Princeton University Press.

Ogden, T. (1986). *The Matrix of the Mind*. NJ: Jason Aronson, Inc.

Reik, T. (1954). *Listening With the Third Ear*. New York: Farrar, Straus and Co.

Rhally, M. (1968). Difficulties in the therapeutic encounter. In J.B. Wheelwright (Ed.), *The Reality of the Psyche.* New York: G.P. Putnam & Sons, pp. 222-234.

Richet, C. (1884). *La Suggestion Mentale et le Calcul des Probabilities. Rev. Phil XVIII, II,* 609-74.

Schmeck, H. (1974). *Immunity, the Double Edged Sword.* New York: Braziller.

Searles, H. (1979). *Countertransference and Related Subjects.* New York: International University Press.

Sheldrake, R. (1984). Mind, memory and archetype: morphic resonance and the collective unconscious. *Psychological Perspectives,* pp. 9-25.

_____. (1981). *A New Science of Life: The Hypothesis of Formative Causation.* Boston: Houghton & Mifflin Company.

_____. (1988). *The Presence of the Past.* London: Collins.

Spitz, R. (1945). Hospitalization: An inquiry into the genesis of psychiatric conditions of early childhood. In R.S.Eissler, A. Freud, H. Hartman & E. Kris (Eds.), *The Psychoanalytic Study of the Child.* New York: International University Press, pp. 53-74.

Spotnitz, H. (1969). *Modern Psychoanalysis of the Schizophrenic Patient.* New York: Grune and Stratton.

Strachey, J. (1934). The nature of the therapeutic action of psychoanalysis. In R. Langs (Ed.), *Classics in Psychoanalytic Technique.* New York: Jason Aronson, Inc., 1981, pp. 351-378.

Sullivan, H. (1954). *The Psychiatric Interview.* New York: W.W. Norton & Company, Inc..

Von Franz, M.-L. (1970). *Puer Aeternus.* Zurich: Spring Publications.

West, M. (1983). *The World Is Made of Glass.* New York: William Morrow Publishers.

Wiesel, Elie. (2000). *And the Sea is Never Full: Memoirs, 1969 – .* New York: Shocken.

Wilhelm, R., & Baynes, C. (1950). *The I Ching: Or the Book of Changes.* NJ: Princeton University Press.

Winnicott, D. (1935). The manic defense. In D.W. Winnicott (Ed.), *Through Pediatrics to Psychoanalysis.* New York: Basic Books, 1975, pp. 129-145.

_____. (1960). The theory of the parent-infant relationship. In D.W. Winnicott (Ed.), *The Maturational Process and the Facilitating Environment.* 1965B, pp. 37-56.

_____. (1964). *The Child, the Family and the Outside World.* New York: Pelican Books.

Zukav, G. (1979). *The Dancing Wu Li Masters: An Overview of the New Physics.* New York: Quill.

INDEX

ego-Self relationship 101
ego/Self axis 10, 69
Einstein, Albert 8
Electromagnetism and the Sacred (Fagg)
   14
Eliade, Mircea 28
emergence 26
empathic failure 48
entrainment 14
equilibrium 125
evolutionary feedback 140

F

Fagg, Lawrence
   Electromagnetism and the Sacred 14
fairy tales 16
family therapy 123
   and frame theory 124
   models of 124
father complex 84 —*See also* complex
Faunus 30, 31
fields 8, 112, 140
   and therapeutic setting 109
   and therapeutic system 130
   archetypal 10, 13
   as determinant of trajectories 13
   as shaper of form 14
   biological 9
   electrical 14
   embeddedness in 142
   generating form 13
   gravitational 14
   magnetic 14
   morphogenetic 110
   quantum 113
   relationship with form 11
field interactions 113
field theory
   and archetypes 113
Fordham, Michael 47
form 15

development in the therapeutic
   relationship 7
generation of 6, 7, 124
relationship with field 11
reoccurrence of 110
form-shaping field 14
formative causation 110, 113
frame
   and derivative communication 50
   and special conditions of treatment
     98, 107
   breaks in 50, 108, 128
frame issues
   breaks in ideal frame 37
   in treatment 6
Freud, Sigmund 7, 23, 25, 71
   and Jung 80, 81
   and repetition compulsion 130
   and seduction theory 54
   and sexual libido theory 82
   and therapeutic system 114
*Freud-Jung Relationship: The Other Side
   of Oedipus* (Alexander) 79

G

good enough mother 49
Goodheart, W. 23
Goodwin, Brian 9
   theory of biological form 109
Great Mother 35, 40, 42
Greenacre, P. 25
Guggenbuhl-Craig, Adolph 85

H

Hannah, Barbara 81
Harlow, Harry 46
Healing Hand, The (Majno) 31
healing rites 24, 28
   as archetpally derived mode of cure
     28
healing sites 28, 31

morphogenetic field
   Jungian view of 2
   manifestations in initital interview
      43
   role in therapeutic relatinship 4
   unconscious dyanamics of 4
self-organizing systems 123, 141
Selvini, Mara 127
sexual libido theory 82
Sheldrake, Rupert 9, 14, 26, 115,
   117
   and archetypal form 111
   and formative causation 110
   and morphogenetic fields 110,
      130, 140
   and resonance fields 140
   and resonance patterns 110
   and formative causation 113
   and theory of biological form 109
special conditions of treatment 120
Spitz, R. 46
splinter self 58
stable attractor 13
Strachey, J. 43
Structure and Dynamics of the Psyche
   (Jung) 72, 91
Sullivan, H. 23
Symbols of Transformation (Jung) 80
systems theory
   and therapeutic setting 141

T

temenos 91, 98
Theory of the Parent/Infant Relation-
   ship, The (Winnicott) 45
therapeutic field 141
therapeutic frame
   and special treatment conditions 25
therapeutic hold
   breakdown of 49
   breaks in and trauma 50

therapeutic setting
   and secure frame dread 41
   and unconscious experience 120
   creation of 27
therapeutic system
   and morphogenetic resonance 111
   and unconscious communication
      124
   as a field 113, 130
Thompson, D'Arcy 14
Tiber Island 29
trajectory
   of therapeutic system 13
transcendence 8
trauma 25, 41, 48, 91, 106, 107
   and death anxiety 42
   and frame issues 37
   and recreation in analysis 25
   and relationship to Self 108
   and secure frame 38
   and uroboric mother 37
Two Essays on Analytical Psychology
   (Jung) 85

U

unconscious 30, 42, 43, 59
   and derivative communication 65
   as guide to therapeutic process 44
   curative aspects of 39
   terrifying aspects of 39
   unconscious contents 58
   unconscious dynamics 57
unconscious communication 12, 23,
   54, 55, 66, 77, 85, 108, 119,
   120, 124, 128, 130
   and family systems 127
   and initial interview 27, 44, 86
   as perturbation in family system
      134
unconscious dynamics 4, 5–*See also*
   Self: unconscious dyanamics of